DEA+H IN SALEM

THE PRIVATE LIVES BEHIND THE 1692 WI+CH HUNT

DIANE E. FOULDS

Guilford, Connecticut

For Joe

Distributed by NATIONAL BOOK NETWORK

Library of Congress Cataloging-in-Publication Data is available on file.

ISBN 978-0-7627-8497-4

Printed in the United States of America

C⊕NTENTS

PREFACE

A Cauldron of Discontent—
The Pressures That Drove
a Tranquil Village to
Combustion

It was all Mary Taylor could do to get by. Impoverished and probably pregnant, she had a baby at the breast and a houseful of children. Her name surfaces in the Massachusetts records in 1692, after her neighbor Mary Marshall reports her to the authorities. Taylor would join the ranks of more than one hundred and fifty arrested that year for witchcraft. At her subsequent hearing, her story spills out.

It seems that a local man, William Hooper, was in need of a wet nurse. He dropped his child off, but on this day, Taylor wasn't up to the job. They quarreled, and a short time after, the man turned up dead. His family members procured several cases of wine for the funeral, but it mysteriously vanished. Then their house caught fire and burned to the ground, with Hooper's body laid out in the parlor.

Mary Marshall harbored the suspicion that Taylor had killed her prickly customer, made off with the wine, and set his house ablaze. The magistrate would pummel the hapless matron with angry questions, but no one seemed to find anything at all unusual in the fact that this forty-year-old Reading goodwife would have to nurse other people's children to make ends meet.

Her plight, a detail buried in the court archives, is a poignant reminder of how difficult day-to-day living was in seventeenth-century Massachusetts. Faced with crop failures and hostile neighbors, toiling under a class system only slightly less rigid than it was in medieval England, and subjected to Indian ambushes, plagues, house fires, and a broken court system, tempers were quick to fray.

Early death was as frequent as it was unexpected, whether from smallpox, tomahawk, childbirth, or falling from a tree. The smallest spark incited panic. When Salem reached the combustion point in 1692, the most suggestible members of society—children and adolescent girls—were the first to succumb.

The usual story is that the witch hunt was started in the home of Reverend Samuel Parris, when his nine-year-old daughter and twelve-year-old niece dabbled in fortune-telling—a raw egg dropped into a glass of water formed the image of a coffin.[1] The two girls did suffer a breakdown, but what triggered it remains uncertain. Since the local doctor couldn't come up with a medical explanation, he attributed their condition to witchcraft. The panic spread to other households, and before eleven months had passed, twenty persons were put to death.

The contagion would engulf at least twenty-two Massachusetts villages, culminating in the arrest of over one hundred and fifty people. Fifty-nine were tried, thirty-one convicted, and nineteen hanged. One stubborn elder, Giles Corey, was pressed to death for refusing to stand trial. At least eight others, including two young children and an aged widow, died in the squalid prisons.

Though suspects were interrogated throughout the year, the actual trials began in June. Once newly installed English monarchs William and Mary had restored the colony's charter, Massachusetts would again be mostly free to rule itself. To handle the burgeoning witchcraft caseload, Governor William Phips quickly formed a temporary tribunal, the Court of Oyer and Terminer.

Much of the testimony drew on spectral evidence, the impassioned claims that witches were sending their spirits out to wreak mischief on hapless innocents. Most of the suspects admitted to the crime, especially once it became clear that confessors were not as likely to be hanged. By October, so many improbable candidates had been named as witches that the public grew skeptical. Unsure of what to do, Governor Phips halted the proceedings and called on higher-ups in London for advice. By the time a missive arrived in the summer of 1693 insisting he use his own judgment, the trials were over. Farmhouses had been stripped or shuttered, fields left untilled, children orphaned or consigned to foster homes. More important, a community had lost its mooring.

For all its drama, the witch hunt flared and fizzled in under a year, fed by tensions and external pressures that had been building for more than two decades. The Massachusetts government would admit its terrible mistake in 1697, paying restitution to the victims' families. Yet nearly three centuries would pass before all of the victims' names were cleared, a delay that may have helped preserve its dark hold on the American conscience.

With the distance of time, the episode seems to grow more incomprehensible, even as historians add new insights to the growing repository of witch hunt lore.

How could it have happened? The impulse is to condense a frustratingly complicated event into a single neat answer. Many try to grasp the whole picture or track the events chronologically. Yet each personal story, like Mary Taylor's, is part of the mosaic, a microcosm of a fragile Massachusetts society in the throes of transition. Taken together, these biographies form a psychological profile of the Massachusetts Bay at the close of the seventeenth century.

Drawn from a multitude of primary and secondary sources, each begins with the individual's name, place of residence, and age in 1692, the year the witch hunt occurred. Where possible, an attempt has been made to throw light on the personal circumstances and pressures that compelled each person to respond as they did.

CHAPTER I

THE ACCUSERS

Prayers, chores, church. They were the pillars of New England life, a rhythm broken only by an unexpected visitor, the discovery of a wild berry patch, or a juicy bit of gossip. The rest was wearily predictable.

Before she was ten, an English girl in seventeenth-century Massachusetts would have been rigorously trained in the domestic arts. She passed hours at the butter churn and the spinning wheel, wrestled the laundry in the chill of the nearest stream, hauled the water, fed the chickens, swept the floor, collected the eggs, emptied the chamber pot, and milked the cow. It was a female world, confined to respectful titles, proper dress, and virtuous thoughts. The men and boys vanished at dawn to spend the day hunting, herding, or haying.

If she was fortunate, a girl had sisters to share the intimacies, hand-me-downs, and chores. Many were not. Wars and plagues left countless seventeenth-century girls orphaned and homeless, with no alternative but to serve others as domestic servants. For them, days were passed sweating over another family's household, with little to show for it but a bowl of porridge, a change of clothes, and a place to sleep.

A tenuous wall separated them from the wilderness. Wolves and elk roamed beyond the tree line;

robust people fell dead for no apparent reason, and sinister spirits preyed upon the complacent or weak-willed. Every village elder told of the children carried off by Indians or simply hacked to death along with their families. The pastors warned of hellfire and damnation, leaving many a terrified child to lie awake at night, fearing for her soul. Perhaps most troubling of all was a girl's utter powerlessness to alter the course of her own life.

As a child, she ranked near the bottom of the social scale; as a female child, she was virtually invisible. For the rest of her life, her very survival would depend on the charity of men. Fending for herself was not feasible. Since they couldn't vote, it wasn't customary for women to own land or run businesses. The few who did were looked upon with disapproval. Only boys were schooled outside the home. A girl's only chance to achieve a measure of respectability and financial security in her life was to marry. How well she married had a lot to do with her family's social station and the size of her dowry. Servants and war orphans could only hope for God's blessing and a shred of luck. With luck, her husband would not beat her. With luck, he would inherit property and govern his vices. With luck, he might even prove companionable.

With so much resting on intangibles, it's little wonder that the young women of Salem Village indulged in occasional fortune-telling. How suspenseful this ritual must have been, how frightening to summon a portent of death. If caught at this forbidden game, they faced punishment at home and possibly a humiliating dressing-down at church before the eyes of the entire village. So what a relief it must have been in 1692 when a physician cleared them of guilt by proclaiming them the victims of sorcery. What a lark to willfully turn things on their heads at the Sunday service, to shriek and rave with total impunity.

To look more convincingly "afflicted," some cut or bit themselves until they bled. Others threw themselves fainting and convulsing to the floor. Being bewitched was a team sport that gave them license to break rules. They interrupted sermons, hurled insults at pastors, tore pages out of the Scriptures, and pointed accusing fingers at feeble elders, some of whom they hardly knew. Girls who had been bored and neglected now found themselves pitied and awed, even deferred to, until the game got out of hand. Having set the flood in motion, they could no longer steer its course. Before they knew it, these distracted children were sending innocents to their deaths.

By the time the furor had run its course, more than seventy men, women, and children had stepped forward as witnesses or accusers. What had started with a few tremulous girls evolved into a cathartic exorcism engaging every segment of the community. As the following profiles reveal, the pent-up hostilities that fueled it went far deeper than anyone might have guessed.

ELIZABETH BOOTH, SALEM, 18

Her father, a woodworker, had died when she was eight years old. Her mother soon remarried, but just four years later, Elizabeth was fatherless again. Now the family struggled to stave off destitution. By the time the witchcraft episode broke out in 1692, Elizabeth was eighteen, old enough to marry, and still busy helping her twice-widowed mother feed the family. Living on the outskirts of Salem Village, she and her mother had two more to feed: her brother, George, and her younger sister, Alice. Worried about her marital prospects and possibly fearful that her neighbors would look askance at the death of two patriarchs in quick succession, Elizabeth cast her lot with the afflicted.

In late May, she joined them in heaping blame on a Marblehead fisherman's wife, Wilmot Reed. She railed relentlessly against John and Elizabeth Proctor and Sarah, their fifteen-year-old daughter. Later she would add Goody Proctor's sister to the list, as well as Proctor's two teenage sons, William and Benjamin. In early August, she swore that her stepfather's ghost had appeared before her and told her that Goody Proctor, a healer, had murdered him out of spite, being incensed that the Booths had not summoned her sooner, when he first became ill. The testimony suggests that Elizabeth harbored feelings of guilt about her stepfather's death.

By September, her fourteen-year-old sister, Alice, had joined the chorus of accusers, as had sixteen-year-old Elizabeth Wilkins, who two months earlier had married her brother, George. The new bride may have hoped that joining the "afflicted" might deflect attention from the embarrassing fact that she was four months pregnant. To inspire further pity, the Booth girls proclaimed that fifty specters had flooded into their rural home for a devil's communion of bread and wine. Giles Corey acted as the ringleader, they said, at the head of thirteen witches who clamored for them to surrender. Yet despite their urgings, the Booth girls had refused.

If Elizabeth feared that the women in her family were good candidates for victimization, she must have prided herself for acting as she did, because ultimately, no family member was accused. Two years after the trials ended, her resourcefulness paid off again. She married Israel Shaw in Salem and started a family. Her sister, Alice, would find a husband five years later.

Her sister-in-law would not do so well. In 1696 she and her husband, George, were called into court to face charges of premarital fornication. George, who came alone due to his wife's illness, confessed to the charge and paid their fines, forty shillings each, plus court costs. He himself died within a few years, as did their child. When his widow later joined the Salem church, she expressed remorse for the fornication, but neglected to mention that she had willfully accused innocent neighbors of witchcraft.

Perhaps the church forgot to ask.

RICHARD CARRIER, ANDOVER, 18

He was conceived in sin, the firstborn of a willful Andover farm girl and her Welsh lover. Though Martha Allen married Thomas Carrier two months before Richard's birth in 1674, the truth of her circumstances was well-known, as she had openly named Carrier the father of her child.

Richard grew up on the northern fringe of Billerica, within walking distance of Wamesit, a village of peaceful Indians who had adopted the Christian faith. Fraternizing with these natives, whom the English considered the devil's children, would have further sullied his reputation. Initially, Richard's family grew and prospered. But when he was fifteen, their luck ran out. Perhaps because the English authorities had rescinded all land titles, the Carriers were forced to move to Andover to live with Martha's parents. Trial testimony suggests a proud young man who was quick to anger. When his cousin, Allen Toothaker, opposed his mother's stance in a boundary dispute, Richard grabbed him by the hair and threw him to the ground.

A few months after his mother's arrest on charges of witchcraft, the now eighteen-year-old Richard was rounded up with his brother Andrew, who was three years younger. At first they refused to cooperate, but the magistrates took them out of the interrogation room and ordered them "tied neck & heels," a method of restraint that involved being strung up by the hands and feet, facing down, forcing the blood to their heads. Now Richard changed his tune. He readily confessed to signing Satan's book, attending witch meetings, and giving the devil permission to torment other villagers.

Pressured further, he accused several jailed suspects and, reluctantly, his imprisoned mother and aunt, Mary Toothaker, along with her husband, Roger, who had died a month before in Boston prison. Thereafter Richard joined the accusers with reckless abandon, convinced, perhaps, that it was his only chance at survival. He named several individuals who were awaiting trial but avoided accusing anyone new.

Within weeks, his sister Sarah, who was only seven, and his ten-year-old brother, Thomas Jr., would also be thrown in prison and questioned by the magistrates, leaving his father to bring them food and clothing and tend the youngest, four-year-old Hannah. Mindful by now that those who confessed were spared, Richard may very well have coached his younger sister and brother on what to say in court, as each of them obediently confessed to the usual activities; all of them, except Andrew, accused their mother. Sarah held the judges in thrall, describing how her mother had come to her in the shape of a cat. How did she know the cat was her mother? It had told her. Richard could not save the life of his uncompromising mother, but he and his siblings were released from jail early in 1693.

The same year, he married Elizabeth Sessions, who had lost her reputation after bearing the illegitimate child of William Bixby, in whose home she had worked as a servant. In 1703 they left Andover for good to start a new life in Colchester, Connecticut. Richard had five children by Elizabeth. After her death in 1704, he married Thankful Brown and fathered another four. He died in Colchester in 1749 at age seventy-five, having run a prosperous farm and sawmill.

SARAH CHURCHILL, SALEM, 25?

She was one of only three accusers (Mary Warren and Mary Watkins were the others) brave enough to admit that she had faked her seizures.

Like so many of the afflicted girls, Sarah Churchill (spelled Churchwell in some documents) was baptized in the terrors of Indian warfare. Her grandfather, John Bonython, was a prominent property owner in Saco, Maine. When Indians attacked in 1680, the family abandoned their impressive home over the Saco River and fled to Major William Phillips's garrison house on the opposite shore. Sarah, who was eight, was one of about fifty mostly women and children who took refuge inside. The next morning, the Indians sacked and burned the houses on the opposite bank, including her grandfather's. Then they set fire to Phillips's mills, hoping to lure the garrison's defenders out. When that failed, they attempted to torch the garrison itself. Several were wounded in the gunfire, including Sarah's grandfather, though no one was killed. In the morning, the Indians withdrew.

Sarah fled with her parents, Arthur and Eleanor Churchill, to Marblehead, Massachusetts, where her grandfather would later die of his wounds. She then moved to Salem Village (now Danvers), where a relative, Nathaniel Ingersoll, ran a tavern.

By 1692 she was twenty-five. Her once prominent family having fallen on hard times, she was reduced to working as a lowly maidservant, employed in the home of George Jacobs Sr., a strong-willed elder. Her marital prospects looked dim, as she could no longer entice suitors with the promise of an inheritance or even a dowry.

When the community erupted in witchcraft, Sarah's afflicted friends, including her eighteen-year-old relative Mary Walcott, may have pressured her into joining their ranks. She seemed hesitant. At first she exhibited the usual symptoms, but they cleared up. Noticing that she had recovered, Mercy Lewis asserted that Sarah had succumbed to the devil's bidding (why else would he cease to torment her?). Mercy then claimed that she had persuaded Sarah to confess and that, when George Jacobs Sr. had learned of it, he had beaten Sarah "most cruelly" with his wooden canes. Sarah admitted that her afflictions had left her "unable to doe her service as formerly" and that Jacobs had hurled abuse at her, calling her "bitch witch" and other derogatory names. He and his granddaughter, Margaret Jacobs, had forced her to sign the devil's book. Sarah's words prompted a chorus of charges, and soon Jacobs and his granddaughter were in prison. But Sarah's accusation ultimately backfired. Soon she found herself among the accused and she landed in jail. In June she confessed again, hoping that this time she would win the magistrates' mercy. She did.

Though she accused George Jacobs, Ann Pudeator, and Bridget Bishop, she retracted her words later, saying she had lied when threatened with the prospect of being thrown in the dungeon. The problem was getting the authorities to believe her.

"If I told Mr. Noyes but once I had set my hand on the Book he would believe me," she is recorded as saying, "but if I told the truth and said I had not set my hand to the Book a hundred times he would not believe me."

In 1709 Sarah moved to Berwick, Maine. At the age of thirty-seven, she married a weaver, after paying a court fine for fornication. She also received a portion of her inheritance. Though the family estate was long gone, her grandfather had left a piece of Saco land to her mother. Sarah and her husband sold it for fifty pounds sterling. She would never again reach the level of wealth that she had enjoyed with her grandfather, though she outlived her husband. She was still alive at the age of sixty-four, but she disappeared from the records thereafter.

Elizabeth Hubbard, Salem Village, 17

She was a neighbor of Betty Parris and Abigail Williams, whose panicked convulsions had ignited the crisis. She would be one of the first to exhibit signs of diabolical possession, eventually accusing twenty-nine individuals, fifteen of whom would be executed.

"Betty" was born in 1675, just as King Philip's War was erupting across New England, scattering English settlers and leaving thousands dead or wounded. Whole villages were burned to the ground, their residents massacred. It is unknown what became of Betty's family or who stepped in to raise her. We do know that she was living in Boston as the indentured servant of a distant relative, Isaac Griggs. But in 1689 Griggs and his wife died. So at fourteen, Betty was orphaned once again.

Griggs's father, Dr. William Griggs, paid the executor of his son's will for the remaining time on Betty's indenture. Soon after, she began to work for Dr. Griggs, moving with him and his wife from Gloucester to Salem Village. An aging physician, Griggs was struggling to establish his practice. With his own children grown and gone, the brunt of the chores fell on Betty. How awed she would have been to learn that Reverend Parris's daughter and niece had fallen under Satan's spell; how excited to see the drama unfold at close range.

At seventeen, Betty was old enough to testify under oath. That fact may have spurred village leaders to try the accused witches in court. Betty's own motivations are less clear. Perhaps she joined the accusers to relieve the boredom, perhaps to please Dr. Griggs. Of the twenty-nine people she incriminated, at least one of them, Elizabeth Proctor, was a medical practitioner. Griggs had complained of her incompetence. Betty might have reasoned that by accusing her and thereby eliminating a rival, she would win her master's praise.

As a bonus, her testimony exempted her from household chores through the summer and fall, though she was hardly idle. She spent the time filing forty witchcraft charges and giving testimony thirty-two times. Yet when it was over, Betty Hubbard seemed to emerge from her ordeal unscathed. She moved to Gloucester, possibly to live with one of Dr. Griggs's married children, where she married John Bennett and had four children.

If she lived to regret her deeds, there is no indication of it. What *has* survived is the testimony of a neighbor, James Kettle. On a visit to Dr. Griggs's house, he ran into Betty, who admitted that she and Mary Walcott had played hooky from church to visit James Holton, who was suffering stomach cramps. His pain, she told him, was the devious work of John and Elizabeth Proctor and their two children.

As if to prove it, Betty and Mary fell writhing to the floor, claiming the Proctors' specters were attacking them. Later Betty hitched a ride on the back of Clement Coldrum's horse. Go faster, she urged him, as the woods are full of devils. "There," she said, pointing, "and there they be." Though he couldn't see anything that remotely resembled devils, Coldrum kicked his horse into a gallop. Thinking it strange that she looked so unruffled, he asked if she wasn't afraid of Lucifer. "Oh no," Betty said, she could talk to the devil as easily as she could to him.

JOHN INDIAN, SALEM VILLAGE, AGE UNKNOWN

When Reverend Samuel Parris moved his household from Barbados to Boston in 1680, three slaves came with him: a woman named Tituba, John Indian, and a boy. Tituba was a brown-skinned native of "New Spain," which could have meant southern Florida or the islands off Georgia, the Caribbean, or South America. John Indian's racial background is unknown, though the boy was an African who died of unknown causes at the age of fifteen.

Some sources suggest that John and Tituba were married in 1689, the year the Parris family moved to Salem Village. While Tituba cooked and kept house, John and the "Negro lad" did the heavy work, tilling the fields and splitting wood. As slaves, they endured whippings if found idle. In his 1692 writings, Captain Nathaniel Cary, a Charlestown shipbuilder, recorded an encounter with John Indian in Salem Village. The slave showed him his scars, saying witchcraft had caused them. To Cary the marks "seemed as if they had long been there."

When Tituba became entwined in the witch crisis that February, John kept his distance. They had everything to lose. The couple could be cast into the wilderness, sold, or worse; some colonies burned slaves alive for crimes against their owners. John probably urged his wife to submit and show contrition, which she did. Tituba would become Salem's first accused witch to break down and confess. She wove fabulous tales of covens and bewitchings, apologized, even proclaimed her love for her alleged victim, Betty Parris. Then she strategically allied herself with the growing contingent of victims. John banded with her, probably hoping that victimhood would improve their chances of survival. He was an impassioned sufferer, issuing spectacular accusations and falling into dramatic trances and contortions. At the Salem Village parsonage, his anguish was so acute that Reverend Parris could not keep his eyes on his note-taking, writing later that John Indian had fallen into "a violent fit that 3 men & the Marshall could not without exceeding difficulty hold him."

While the witchcraft examinations were under way in May, John was serving customers at Ingersoll's Tavern when Captain Cary stopped in to meet with Abigail Williams. "To him we gave some Cyder," Cary wrote in his diary. It was then that John Indian showed him his scars.

He continued to name witches, as did Tituba, who confessed to her sorcery, then recanted, finally languishing in prison until April of 1693. Though the first to confess, she was the last to be released. Since Parris refused to pay her jail fees, she remained in the filthy cell for thirteen months until an unknown person, possibly a slave trader, paid the seven pounds due. Her fate is unknown, as is John's.

MERCY LEWIS, SALEM VILLAGE, 19

At least nine of the witch hunt's "afflicted" girls had been traumatized at a young age by Indian warfare. When Mercy Lewis was barely three, a war party struck the Falmouth, Maine, hamlet her grandparents had settled in the 1640s. On an August day in 1676, warriors descended on the settlement, whooping and screeching. They torched houses, maimed livestock, and went on a killing spree, abducting more than twenty women and children, many of them Mercy's relatives.

Her parents and the local minister, Reverend George Burroughs, gathered her up and fled to a Casco Bay island. After English troops brought them to safety, the Lewises moved south to Salem. There they were joined by an uncle, who would die a few months later. When the Indian hostilities subsided in 1683, Mercy's family returned to Falmouth, rebuilding their home and scraping by; there was scarcely enough grain or corn to contribute their share of Reverend Burroughs's salary.

In September of 1689, the Indians returned. This time, her parents were slain. Mercy, now sixteen, became a servant in Reverend Burroughs's home. After his wife's death, Burroughs moved his family to Wells, but Mercy joined other refugees migrating down the coast to Salem Village, where she became a domestic in the home of Thomas Putnam.

She probably shared her horrific experiences with the Putnam children. When nine-year-old Ann Putnam was seized with convulsions, Mercy succumbed to them, too. By this time, she was nineteen. Being older than the other girls, she exercised a certain seniority. When Ann Putnam accused Nehemiah Abbott, Mercy insisted she was mistaken. When the other girls withdrew their claims against Mary Easty, Mercy did not. Having known Reverend Burroughs and the Hobbs family in Falmouth, her opinions of them were given more credibility.

Not surprisingly, Mercy's dark visions bore a close resemblance to Indian warfare. She felt as if she were being strangled and jabbed by hot irons. A strange force seemed to push her into the fire. In early May, she described seeing Burroughs's specter. In what sounded like a girl's romantic fantasy, she testified that the minister had swept her up to a high mountaintop, where he promised her all the kingdoms of earth if she would only sign the devil's book. When she refused, he turned abusive, threatening to break her neck and impale her on a hundred pitchforks.

On May 20, Mercy took to her bed, as if reliving the trauma she must have experienced during the Indian attacks. "Dear Lord, receive my soul," she uttered. "Lord, let them not kill me quite." She regained her senses long enough to gasp that Goody Easty had sworn to kill her by midnight. Then she collapsed into convulsions. "Pray for the salvation of my soul," she cried, "for they will kill me." Though Goody Easty was promptly taken into custody, her specter continued to plague Mercy, beckoning her to the grave with the vision of a corpse's winding-sheet.

After the witch hunt's conclusion, the guilt-ridden young woman moved to Greenland, a village outside

Portsmouth, New Hampshire, to live with her aunt. Perhaps she felt the need to distance herself from the people she had wronged. In 1695 she bore a child out of wedlock, but six years later, her life took a turn for the better. She married Charles Allen and moved with him to Boston.

Elizabeth Parris, Reading, 9

If the origins of the Salem witch hunt could be traced to a single individual, it would be Elizabeth Parris, known by her nickname Betty. As the daughter of Reverend Samuel Parris, she was looked to as a model of virtue. Yet like a balloon in a blacksmith's shop, she could only take so much heat.

Born in Boston, Betty was the second of three children. Her family left the safety of the city and moved to Salem Village when she was six, bringing with them her twelve-year-old cousin, Abigail Williams, and at least two slaves, Tituba and John Indian. Abigail's presence probably served as a constant reminder to Betty of the danger of living in remote inland settlements. Salem Village was dangerously close to Indian country, where the bloodcurdling whoops of marauding warriors could fill the air at any moment.

There were other anxieties, too. A cloud of discontent was growing against Betty's father. Many villagers disagreed with his strict policy on church membership, which excluded most of them from baptism and communion. They expressed their bitterness by reneging on their pledges of firewood, grain, and money.

Though only nine, Betty would have sensed the discontent. Reverend Parris was a strict taskmaster, demanding discipline from his parishioners. His wife, when not bedridden, acted properly subservient. His children probably feared him, while Tituba would have treated him with humble deference. In his sermons, Parris warned of the spiritual battle between the saved and the damned. Satan and his wicked accomplices, he preached, are "the grand enemy of the Church," bent on its destruction. It was after one such blistering rant that Betty and Abigail began acting strangely. They crouched under chairs, twisted their arms and legs in unnatural positions, and cried out as if they were being choked and bitten.

If Betty's father had previously been remote, now he was a fixture at her bedside, praying and fasting. For weeks her symptoms festered. She barked and convulsed, babbling unintelligibly and falling into trances. After Dr. Griggs diagnosed Betty's and Abigail's fits as bewitchment, her father demanded answers. Who was tormenting her?

Having caused such a tumult, there could be no turning back. She had to name someone, so she chose Tituba. Under further questioning, Betty blamed two local misfits, Sarah Good and Sarah Osborne. The convulsions spread to other girls in the neighborhood, and soon Betty was leading a chorus of afflicted women and girls. It may have comforted her to know that others were sharing the spotlight and—if they were found out—the consequences. When the magistrates formally interrogated them, they mimicked the suspects' every gesture, like puppets yanked on invisible strings.

But weeks of such antics proved exhausting. Her mother began to fear for Betty's health, so in March, it was decided that Betty would pay an extended visit to a family friend in Salem, Stephen Sewall. Soon her symptoms ceased.

The witch trials continued without her, perhaps sparing her the guilt that would leave an indelible stain on the lives of other accusers, such as Ann Putnam Jr. In 1710, at the age of twenty-seven, Betty married Benjamin Baron in Sudbury, Massachusetts. They had five children. Betty Parris lived to the age of seventy-seven, surviving her husband by six years.

ANN PUTNAM JR., SALEM VILLAGE, 12

The eldest child of a Salem Village family, Ann Putnam was raised in a climate of sorrow and bitterness. Both parents, Thomas and Ann Carr Putnam, felt that they had been cheated out of their rightful inheritances; to make matters worse, it seemed as if a curse had laid its hand upon her mother: She had lost seven newborns. Yet instead of confronting the family members responsible for their financial misfortunes, Ann's parents channeled their frustrations into Salem's witch hunt, with Ann as their pawn.

Though only twelve, she would become one of the most obsessive accusers, claiming specters were biting and pinching her. Her mother sometimes joined in the frenzied hysterics, lashing out at innocent neighbors and upbraiding those who disagreed with their friend and ally, Reverend Samuel Parris.

Ann's father initiated almost half of the twenty-one formal complaints filed against suspected witches, feeding their names and alleged crimes to his daughter. Ann's own name appeared more than four hundred times in the legal documents. Before it was over, she would accuse nineteen and see eleven hang. Yet it did the family little good. Ultimately, Reverend Parris was ousted and the Putnams disgraced. Ann and Thomas Putnam died, heavily in debt, within two weeks of each other in 1699, leaving Ann Jr. to care for her nine younger siblings.

In adulthood, she would seek forgiveness for her role in the witch hunt. While joining the Salem Village church in 1706, Ann stood quietly before the congregation as Reverend Parris's successor, Joseph Green, recited a solemn statement acknowledging her guilt and expressing her wish to be "humbled before God." It had been "a great delusion of Satan" that deceived her in that sad time, the statement said. She had acted "ignorantly," yet "without anger, malice, or ill-will to any person," and wished only to "lie in the dust" for the wrong she had done Rebecca Nurse and her two sisters. That wish would be granted. Nine years later, Ann Putnam Jr. died unmarried at the age of thirty-five.

MARGARET RULE, BOSTON, 17

Of the Maine refugees, she was the last to claim that she was being accosted by witches. Margaret Rule, like Sarah Churchill before her, had fled Saco in the 1680s, when the settlement suffered Indian raids.

She was the oldest daughter of Emma and John Rule, a respectable and financially comfortable mariner living in Boston's North End. Her torments started in 1693, as the Salem witch hunt was winding down. She had quarreled with a Boston matron, a magical healer who had been jailed for witchcraft. The harsh words had left Margaret shaken; the next morning, in the middle of a church service, the girl was seized with convulsions so severe that she couldn't walk and had to be carried home.

Mercy Short, who was also living in Boston, might have planted the idea in Margaret's mind, as their sufferings were virtually identical. Indeed, Cotton Mather wrote that the symptoms of one resembled "the full History of the other."

Mather took his neighbor and young parishioner into his home to watch her more closely, as he had Mercy Short, keeping meticulous records of her condition. Like Mercy, Margaret described the devil as "a short and Black Man." She experienced the same pinches and pinpricks and accused a neighbor of bewitching her. But Mather, who by now was well versed in the ways of traumatized young women, discouraged her parents from filing charges. Margaret's ailments would better be cured, he insisted, through fasting and prayer. Though she was "extream weak and faint," Mather wrote, and though it took several weeks, recover she did.

SUSANNAH SHELDON, SALEM VILLAGE, 18

She was less than two years old when a band of Indians burst upon the fortified garrison house where she and her parents were holed up in Black Point (now Scarborough), Maine. They survived the attack, but the memory of that 1675 event left a psychic scar. The following day, the warriors fell upon the nearby village of Dunston, killing nine men, including Susannah's uncle. Despite anguished pleas for help, local military commander Captain Joshua Scottow forbade his troops from going out to rescue the trapped men, fearing it would leave other settlers vulnerable. Though he would defend his decision in court, his reputation never recovered.

Susannah grew up in a household that probably seethed with resentment for the man. While Scottow was still in court, the Indians struck again. This time the Sheldons fled, but they returned to Black Point in the early 1680s, as did Scottow, now a close friend of the former Salem Village pastor, Reverend George Burroughs.

When hostilities flared again in 1688, the Sheldons left Black Point for good, relocating to Salem Village. Their trials weren't over. In 1690 Susannah's twenty-four-year-old brother, Godfrey, was killed in battle. A year later, her sixty-eight-year-old father died when a cut in his leg became infected. So when the witch hunt broke out in the early months of 1692, Susannah was living in a family brutalized by war: her widowed mother, her brother Ephraim, and four sisters.

In late April she was seized with a "spectral vision." She was in the Salem meetinghouse when the apparition of Philip English, a wealthy French-born merchant, stepped over his pew and pinched her. Other visions followed. She professed to see witch suspects suckling pigs, snakes, yellow birds, and black cats. They choked and struck her to keep her from eating, and the corpses of their victims turned "As Red As blood." By June Susannah's torments had taken on a physical component. She spoke of "invisible hands" stealing a saucer from the jury room. Witnesses told of specters repeatedly tying her wrists with a cord, as the Indians had done in Maine.

Fatherless and uprooted, her frenzied descriptions likely reflected her mental state. Though Susannah gave formal testimony in only a few cases, she would ultimately bear witness against twenty-four individuals.

In the trials' aftermath, Captain Scottow published a history in which he referred to Indian chiefs as "Satan's Emissaries" working in league with witches. Susannah must have internalized the notion. Once her testimony was no longer required, she fled Salem Village as she had Black Point, moving to Providence, Rhode Island, to live with a cousin. In 1694 the Providence town council summoned her, possibly to warn her out, since she was a "person of Evill fame" and possibly indigent. There is little record of her subsequent life. She is presumed to have died by 1697, unmarried.

MERCY SHORT, BOSTON, 17

In 1690 Abenaki warriors raided the frontier village of Salmon Falls, New Hampshire (now Berwick, Maine). Clement and Faith Short and three of their nine or ten children were slain. The rest were taken captive, including fifteen-year-old Mercy.

For weeks they were force-marched through the snowy wilderness to Quebec. Along the way, the captors beheaded and scalped a teenage girl as a warning, holding up the trophy and telling the captives that they would share the same fate if they tried to escape. A five-year-old boy was murdered with a hatchet blow to the head, then chopped up before Mercy's eyes. As if such atrocities weren't enough, they tied Mercy's hands and forced her to watch—without flinching—as a Salmon Falls neighbor, Robert Rogers, was stripped, tied to a stake, and tortured to death. As Cotton Mather later described it in his writings, the Abenakis "Danc'd about him, and at every Turn, they did with their knives cut collops of his Flesh, from his Naked Limbs, and throw them with his Blood into his Face."

In 1691 Mercy was ransomed and returned to Massachusetts. When the Salem witch hunt began the following spring, she was in Boston, working as a servant in the home of Margaret Thacher, a wealthy and pious merchant's widow. Mercy probably acted perfectly normal, as if she had fully recovered from her ordeal of the previous year.

But in May, something within her seemed to snap. Sent to Boston jail on an errand, she passed a jailed witch suspect, Sarah Good, who begged her for tobacco. Mercy hurled abuse at the old woman and threw wood shavings in her face. They exchanged curses. Later that evening, Mercy broke down into raving fits. She fainted and screamed and for days was unable to pray or eat. Her minister, Cotton Mather, took her into his home to keep watch on her, on one occasion reading to her from the Bible, only to have her reach over and rip out a page. He prescribed prayer, fasting, and kindness. Neighbors came to see her, youth groups prayed with her, and for a time, her agonies seemed to ease. But during a church service that winter, Mercy's fits returned. This time, she described lurid visions, which Mather meticulously recorded and later published in a tract called *A Brand Plucked From the Burning:* Witches' specters were chaining her, pricking her, forcing poisonous fluids down her throat, and scorching her with fire. Most telling of all, they bore a striking resemblance to Indians.

Mercy began to list the evil-doers assisting these specters; some were respected citizens. Wisely, Mather refused to divulge the names, saying it would cause an uproar and that many were "doubtless innocent." One of the names might have been Mercy's own mistress, Margaret Thacher. Yet the widow was never formally charged, probably because this pious and well-heeled Boston matron was the mother-in-law of one of the trial's main judges, Jonathan Corwin.

Mather, intent on proving that he could "cure" diabolical possessions through prayer, indulged the young woman. Once the witchcraft trials were over, her condition improved; in 1694 she joined Boston's Second Church and married Joseph Marshall, with Cotton Mather officiating. Four years later he would officiate again, this time over her excommunication for adultery.

Whether Mercy ever came to terms with her Indian captivity is questionable. Little has survived about her subsequent life, other than her death before the age of forty.

Martha Sprague, Andover, 16

From mid-July to September of 1692, the focus of the Salem witchcraft crisis shifted to Andover, a more prosperous settlement on Salem Village's northern border. The first to display worrisome signs was Martha Sprague. A few days later, her affliction spread to her thirteen-year-old stepcousin, Rose Foster, and to Abigail Martin, who was nineteen. Most of the accused were their own relatives.

Martha had reasons to be distraught. One of eight children, she was still grieving her father's death in 1690. Her new stepfather was the widower Moses Tyler, a man with a troubled past.

Having spent much of his youth homeless and destitute, he harbored deep resentment against the town's founders. His own father, Job Tyler, had been a squatter in Andover in 1640, before the village was formally settled. When the first proprietors started building their houses in 1644, they evicted him. With the help of a ne'er-do-well moneylender, John Godfrey, Job Tyler purchased his own land, but he would spend years in court battling hopeless lawsuits waged against Godfrey and Andover's blacksmith, Thomas Chandler. In retaliation, Job Tyler charged Godfrey with witchcraft. Moses, who was about nineteen at the time, supported his father in depositions, but the magistrate, Simon Bradstreet, and Andover's minister, Francis Dane, dismissed the case for lack of evidence.

Once again, Moses's father lost his entire Andover property. As a parting blow, he sued Godfrey and

Chandler both, only to lose for the third time. Now homeless, the beleaguered family moved west to Mendon and built a house, which Indians burned to the ground in a 1676 raid.

By 1680 Moses's brother Hopestill and his sister Mary had grown to adulthood and decided to forge out on their own. Perhaps determined to let bygones be bygones, both of them married, settled in Andover, and started families. Moses stayed on in Boxford with his father, no doubt stung that his brother and sister would betray them by moving back to the village.

When the witch uproar spread to Andover in August of 1692, Moses recognized an opportunity. Whether willingly or by coercion, his stepdaughter, Martha Sprague, did his bidding. She promptly came down with the usual symptoms and began naming names. In time, she, Rose, and Abigail would become Andover's most vocal accusers, involving themselves in seventeen cases. Since Martha and the other afflicted girls were too young to file legal papers, Moses Tyler did it for them, citing Martha and Rose as victims. Leading the list were the wives of Andover's original founders. Before the battle was over, virtually all of the Andover-based women in Moses Tyler's extended family also stood accused. All but one of them confessed: his brother Hopestill's widowed mother-in-law, Mary Parker, who was hanged.

Was Martha Sprague trying to win her stepfather's approval? She unflinchingly backed him, just as he had supported his own father, remaining an active accuser into May of 1693. If she ever regretted her role in perpetuating her stepfather's family feud, nothing has survived to suggest it. But she did seem to turn her own life around in later years. She appears in the 1701 records as having married Richard Friend in Andover.

MARY WALCOTT, SALEM VILLAGE, 17

She had come to Ingersoll's Tavern in Salem Village to greet the town's former pastor, the Reverend Deodat Lawson, who was there to look into reports of witchcraft. The tavern's owner, Nathaniel Ingersoll, was a distant relative. But in the middle of the conversation, Mary went pale. A specter had bitten her, she exclaimed. She raised her wrist and showed him the teeth marks.

Her true purpose in meeting Reverend Lawson may have been to communicate that she was joining the accusers. Did she believe the witchcraft rumors, or was she merely in the mood for a little "sport," as a fellow complainant would later say?

We will never know. Unlike so many of the bewitched girls, Mary still lived with her family, though her birth mother had died when she was eight. Her father, Jonathan Walcott, a captain in the local militia, had married Thomas Putnam's sister when Mary was ten. As the fifth of six children (and one of only two girls), she would have been sorely needed to help with domestic chores at home and probably pampered. Her stepmother would bear another seven offspring, two of them girls. Still, Mary's life was relatively stable. She had not lost a father or home or lived through the trauma of Indian warfare, though she would work tirelessly to keep the family fed and clothed.

Like her cousin Ann Putnam Jr., her father supported her accusations. Indeed, he and Thomas Putnam would file sixty-nine witchcraft complaints, the most on record. Acting with her family's blessing, Mary furnished a wealth of damning testimony until the witch hunt was largely over in May of 1693.

Perhaps she believed the cause was righteous. Three years later, she married Isaac Farrar in Salem, moving first to his former home, Woburn, and subsequently to Ashford, Connecticut. They had six children.

MARY WARREN, SALEM, 20

Unlike Mary Walcott, with her large, supportive family, Mary Warren had virtually no one. A servant in the home of John and Elizabeth Proctor, she had fled the Indian bloodshed in Maine with her parents, both of whom subsequently died. Her sole blood relative, a sister, was a deaf-mute.

The Proctor household was hardly the place for emotional hand-wringing. With their eleven children, the family managed a farm, a tavern, and property holdings in Ipswich. Mary would later testify that John and Elizabeth Proctor often quarreled, especially when he had indulged in too much drink. The legal records contain no mention of Mary until her interrogation on April 19, probably because Proctor took a callous attitude to her fits and refused to take her to town. He did take her to Rebecca Nurse's examination in Salem Village, where she joined the other girls in dramatic bouts of wailing and fainting.

In a deposition, Samuel Sibley related that he had run into Proctor on the highway and stopped to chat. Proctor referred to Mary derogatorily as his "jade," insisting the best cure for her fits was a good thrashing.

Because Mary knew that Proctor would beat her if she acted out, her fits ceased until the moment he left her unattended. Her fear of Proctor may have actually pushed her closer to the afflicted group. When the girls accused both of the Proctors of witchcraft that April, they pointed to Mary as the couple's victim. Mary herself would tell of the tongue-lashings that John Proctor inflicted upon her.

He had threatened to "burn her out" of her fit by sticking "hot tongs downe her throat," she exclaimed. During one of her fits, he had shouted, "If ye are afflicted, I wish ye were more Afflicted." When she asked why, he replied, "Because you goe to bring out Innocent persons."

Yet shortly after the Proctors' arrest, Mary herself would end up in jail. In early April, her possession seemed to taper off. To show gratitude, she tacked a note of thanks onto the meetinghouse. The other bewitched girls, perhaps fearing betrayal, declared that if she was feeling better, it must be because she had joined the devil's ranks. Their challenge posed a dilemma.

The Proctors were the closest thing Mary had to parents. If she condemned them, not only would she be out of a home but also destined to suffer more guilt and anguish. Yet to obey them carried the danger of bringing witchcraft suspicions onto herself. In prison, with little else to do, she despaired over the predicament. Four women jailed with her later told of her mental turmoil. "When I was Afflicted," Mary told one, "I thought I saw the Apparission of A hundred persons," but she had been "Distempered," and later she was unsure. When she felt well again, the woman recalled, "Shee Could not Say that Shee saw any of Apparisons at the time Aforesaid."

On the day of Mary's interrogation, Elizabeth Hubbard accused her of claiming that the afflicted girls were simply playacting. The magistrates ignored this invitation to question the girls' credibility. Instead, they listened to Mary's avowals of innocence, while the girls responded by thrashing about in frenzied seizures. Mary convulsed too, flailing and gasping until she was removed from the room. When she was brought back to give testimony about another accused witch, she had more fits and was again taken out for air. For once, the afflictions served as a handy ploy to avoid answering troublesome questions. In a new tactic, the magistrates took her out of the interrogation room and spoke to her in private, but she still evaded their questions.

Later she was questioned in prison, where she both accused others and confessed her own culpability. By April 21, her testimony was so tangled in qualifications that it hardly made sense. The Proctors were guilty, but she wasn't sure they were witches. She had made a mark in the devil's book, but only with the tip of her finger. Three weeks later, her story became even more convoluted. Having denied ever seeing a poppet (a rag doll witches used to cast spells), she now testified that she had stuck a pin into one that Elizabeth Proctor owned. Did she see any others? She said no, then named the witch suspects who had brought her poppets. At this point, the magistrates gave up on her and turned their attentions to what she could tell them about others.

Once released from jail and no longer suspected, she joined the accusers with a vengeance, even making herself bleed from the mouth. Again she railed about the Proctors, stopping just short of branding them witches. Having secured herself on the side of the accusers, it seemed there was nothing she wouldn't say to remain there.

After the trials ended, Mary Warren vanished from the record books. What became of her is unknown.

MARY WATKINS, MILTON, 20S

She was poor and friendless, and though she would confess to lying, her honesty did her little good. Like Mary Warren, Mary Watkins was a servant, in the Milton, Massachusetts, home of Thomas and Sarah Swift. For no discernible reason, she seemed to fall apart, accusing Goody Swift of witchcraft and child murder. The Swifts threatened punishment if she did not retract her words, so Mary apologized. For a time, she seemed to regain her senses. But later that year, she fell into a depression and tried to strangle herself.

It was May of 1693. The witchcraft madness had passed, though it lingered in the public mind. The courts were not anxious to take on new witchcraft cases, since the Salem trials had been largely discredited. So when Mary was called in for questioning about the cause of her afflictions, the jurors questioned her credibility. Dismayed by their skepticism, she changed her tune. She admitted that her accusations were false "and that she had ronged" Goody Swift. Then she accused herself of witchcraft, but the jurors, mindful that she was unstable, refused to indict her. Instead they sent her to jail until she could produce sureties for good behavior. Yet owing to "her deep poverty & want of Friends," she could not muster the funds. So in July, the court dismissed the surety requirement; Judge Samuel Sewall ordered that she be released—as soon as she paid her jail fees.

But even this she could not do. Her small inheritance would have covered the expenses, but her brother-in-law controlled the funds and would not respond to her overtures. Growing weak, and with no one else to turn to, Mary suggested she work the fees off. She had repaid a debt once before through indentured servitude in Virginia, and she could do so again. With the help of a fellow woman prisoner, Susanna Davis of Newbury, she appealed to the Boston jailer, asking if a merchant couldn't be found who would be willing to pay their jail fees in exchange for their labor, seeing as their "friends, relations, and kindred" had slighted them "to extremity."

Why would they abandon their own relative? Perhaps she embarrassed them or was emotionally burdensome. Though little is known about her childhood hardships, her background offers clues. She was the daughter of Margaret and Thomas Watkins, who raised her on the Kennebec River in Maine. Her father died in 1673, after which her mother married Thomas Stevens, who traded furs in the attack-prone wilderness areas north of Casco. In 1688, Indians took him hostage to retaliate against the capture of twenty warriors who had been arrested and marched to Boston for killing English cattle. That might have prompted her family to flee Maine for the safety of Boston.

By August of 1693, she had spent nearly four months in jail, probably suffocating in the heat, stench, and vermin. Without the means to buy food and drink, Mary probably had to beg. But Boston merchant John Winslow stepped forward and paid the two women's fees—four pounds, seven shillings, and six pence. That was the last time she was mentioned in the record books.

ABIGAIL WILLIAMS, SALEM VILLAGE, 12

Of the "afflicted" girls, the most ruthless was probably Abigail Williams, who helped incite the crisis together with her nine-year-old cousin, Betty Parris. An orphan, she was taken in by her uncle, the Reverend Samuel Parris, and became the family's live-in servant. Being the oldest girl, she would have kept busy spinning yarn and doing chores most of the day and into the evenings. She and Betty probably shared a bed and said their usual prayers, hoping not to anger Betty's volatile father.

An emotionally distant man, Parris would have had little inclination to comfort his grief-stricken niece. Nor could his wife offer much solace, being ill much of the time. At a fraught and difficult period in her life, the grieving girl had no one to turn to but young Betty and the family's slaves, Tituba and John Indian, who had worries of their own.

January had been bitterly cold. Tensions in the village were high, and each day was a gloomy repetition of the one before. Food was short, and the firewood was almost gone. Reverend Parris spent long hours writing in the parlor and could not be disturbed. Cooped up in the chilly house, Abigail probably felt restless. Perhaps she told Betty a horrific Indian tale or persuaded Tituba to tell fortunes. Betty may have panicked. There are many theories, but what actually started the two girls' seizures remains a mystery.[1]

Reverend Deodat Lawson visited the parsonage in March and watched with horror as Abigail fell twisting and contorting to the floor. His notes describe her tearing about the room waving her arms, crying "whist, whist, whist," claiming she could see the spirits, or specters, of living people, and that they were pressuring her to sign the devil's book and become a witch. She ran to the hearth, grasped flaming embers with her bare hands, and threw them about the house as if possessed by demons. Perhaps she just needed to vent.

But the result of her antics must have surprised her: Suddenly adults started listening, paying her attention, even showing empathy and esteem. No longer was she a homeless, forgotten little girl. Emboldened, she interrupted the service that Sunday, shouting comments at Reverend Lawson as he stood preaching from the pulpit. As suspects were rounded up and arrested, she feverishly acted the victim, leading a chorus of screaming girls in hysterical outbursts. To prove the harm the accused were inflicting, she pricked and cut herself and taunted her victims, mimicking the turn of a head or the clenching of a fist. Before she was through, Abigail Williams incriminated nine innocent people, some of them virtual strangers.

Though the trials lasted into the fall of 1692, all references to Abigail's shrill theatrics disappeared from the records by July. The last mention of this haunted young woman, besides her death at thirty-seven, appeared in a cryptic letter penned by Reverend John Hale of Beverly. Alluding almost certainly to Abigail, he wrote that a certain afflicted girl had tried "with an egg and a glass to find her future husband's calling, till there came up a coffin, that is, a specter in the likeness of a coffin." Thereafter, Hale wrote, she was "followed with diabolical molestation to her death, and so died a single person."

CHAPTER 2

THE VICTIMS

One of the enduring mysteries of the Salem witch hunt is why some individuals were accused and not others. A dark rationale must have driven the selection process, but through the haze of three hundred years, it can seem wildly random.

Most of the victims were women. Everyone knew that witchcraft was largely a female perversity, but the reasoning stopped there. The over one hundred and fifty people singled out for social and legal ostracism over the course of 1692 included every age, social echelon, and background: rich and poor, young and old, feeble and sharp-witted.[1] In Andover, seventeen alleged witches were identified in a single afternoon sting known as the "touch test." The villagers collected in the meetinghouse, then one by one, the women were blindfolded and led up to two of Salem's writhing girls. If the woman's touch abated the girls' convulsions, it proved that she was guilty. The logic seems to have been that physical contact with an actual witch would draw the evil spirits back out of the victim. So like sheep herded over a cliff, Andover's women were seized, bound, served warrants, and loaded into the back of oxcarts for the four- or five-hour trip to Salem jail, their frantic relatives browbeating them the entire way.

The ulterior reasons for their persecution sometimes surfaced at the trial. Often it was little more than a bad reputation or malicious gossip, repackaged and embroidered over decades. A human frailty or eccentricity might be trotted out as evidence. Sometimes it was the fruit of a protracted family feud, an insult uttered in haste, or a personal indiscretion—like Martha Corey's—that the community refused to forget.

If they confessed to the charges, it was because most were frightened, hungry, and emotionally drained. Some bore the added hardship of being pregnant or deaf. Others were plagued by feelings of unworthiness or pressured by panicked relatives who feared its impact on the rest of the family. Witchcraft, after all, was assumed to be an inherited trait. As often as not, the children, sisters, and spouses of suspected witches were hauled in for safety's sake.

Like most witch hunts, Salem's would amount to a community cleansing, a wholesale purge of antisocial elements by a society struggling to keep its balance. Of the many victims, the twenty-four here represent a special category—the ones who paid with their lives.

BRIDGET BISHOP, SALEM, 50s

Men were transitory in her life, but money was a constant. She was born Bridget Playfer in Norwich, a town on England's southeast coast. In 1660, while in her twenties, she married Samuel Wasselbee and had two children, but all three of them soon died.

In 1664 she sailed for Boston and met a widower, Thomas Oliver. They married and moved to Salem, where Bridget bore a daughter, Christian. From there, Bridget's life started its relentless downhill slide. The couple's squabbling and name-calling became so rancorous that both were served with fines and public whippings. Bridget's face was often bruised or bloodied. Three years into their marriage, they again appeared in court, this time for airing their differences in public, and even worse, on the Sabbath. Her husband's daughter, Mary, paid his fine but not Bridget's, who for lack of money was forced to stand in the marketplace on Lecture Day, wearing a sign on her forehead that broadcasted her offense: "scold," perhaps, or "Sabbath breaker."

If it taught her anything, it was financial self-reliance. She became obsessive over business dealings to the point of quibbling over pennies. In 1682, a local woman named Whatford accused her of swiping a spoon; Bridget retaliated with a good tongue-lashing. Thereafter Whatford claimed that Bridget's specter and that of a certain Goodwife Parker had pulled her down to the beach and tried to drown her. It was a foretaste of what was to come.

Bridget's husband died in 1685 under questionable circumstances, and by 1687 she remarried, this time to the aged Edward Bishop, a co-founder of the Beverly church. She continued doing business, and again was accused of theft. This time the missing article was a brass bearing from Thomas Stacey's mill. When asked where she got the part, she replied that she had found it in the garden. Unfortunately, her daughter, Christian, who had tried to sell it, told a different story: that it had belonged to her late father.

Bridget spent three months in jail waiting for the court to convene. Thomas Stacey, meanwhile, claimed that a remorseful Bridget had begged his forgiveness, an assertion she vehemently denied. As if to defend his father, Stacey's son William, who had testified against Bridget, now reported being bodily seized by evil powers and tossed about his yard.

After marrying Edward Bishop, she had moved into his home on the Ipswich Road in Salem Village and leased her own house in Salem. Later she would turn it into an unlicensed tavern, selling cider made from her apples. A witness would complain about the "drinking and playing at shuffleboard," and the discord it caused local families, not to mention the fact that it left young people "in danger to be corrupted."

In an age when shrinking violets were the feminine ideal, Bridget's late-night hospitality and spirited business ventures offended Puritan sensibilities. Indeed, she was the first to stand trial for witchcraft in 1692. The witnesses were largely men, many of whose complaints came with subtly erotic overtones.

Richard Coman, for example, awoke in his marital bed, with his wife by his side, to find Bridget sprawled on his chest. Samuel Gray and William Stacey both woke to see her specter inserting something into their mouths. John Louder's nocturnal encounter involved Bridget astride his stomach, trying to strangle him. But more worrisome were the damages she caused. Her evil powers, neighbors claimed, had provoked accidents, disease, missing coins, even their children's deaths. John Bly told of the day seven years before when he and his son William had gone to her house to make repairs. Removing a wall, they had discovered poppets, the rag dolls witches used to cast their spells.

The jury quickly pronounced her guilty, after which a physician and nine matrons stripped her to search for physical evidence that she had suckled imps. John Louder, after all, had glimpsed a strange black hog in her yard, as well as a furry chickenlike thing with an eerily human face. No such marks, however, were found.

On the morning of June 10, a procession of guards and mounted soldiers escorted Bridget Bishop in an oxcart to Gallows Hill. A guard patiently waited as she paused on the rung of a ladder, the noose around her neck, declaring her innocence to the throngs below. When she finished, he pushed her off.

GEORGE BURROUGHS, WELLS, 42?

The devil's objective in recruiting witches, as Cotton Mather would explain it, was to bring down the Kingdom of God and replace it with Satan's. By the summer of 1692, Mather had identified Martha Carrier as the woman in line to become queen of hell. Who was to be king? A man of authority, certainly, someone endowed with remarkable physical and spiritual strength. If the beleaguered Salem Villagers sought a candidate whose attributes matched that description, they found him in the Reverend George Burroughs.

According to family legend, he was at the dinner table with his family in Wells, Maine, when they came for him. The guards seized him with few words or explanations, leading him away before he could finish his meal. Some versions tell of thunder and lightning exploding overhead, overturning trees along the trail as the horsemen escorted their prisoner to Salem.

Though small in stature, in almost every other respect Burroughs was extraordinary, one of only two clergymen brave enough to serve in the perilous outreaches of coastal Maine. The other, Reverend Shubael Dummer, would be slain in 1692 when a Penobscot band assaulted York, massacring fifty and abducting a hundred others. Handsome, learned, and articulate, his physical and emotional strength was legendary. Though he was reputed to be short-tempered with his wife, he was fearless in battle. To top it off, he was a Harvard-educated minister.

One accuser, eighteen-year-old Mary Lacey Jr., described him as "a pretty little man," which suggests he did not lack sex appeal. Indeed, he never stayed single for long. Among the few things his parishioners could criticize about the twice-widowed pastor was his tendency to remarry a bit too quickly. His second wife, Sarah Ruck Hathorne, was probably the young and presumably desirable widow of the late Captain William Hathorne, a dashing military officer and war casualty whose older brother, Judge John Hathorne, would preside over the witch trials.

To be labeled the ringleader of Salem's witches, there must have been something about Burroughs that inspired loathing; his peripatetic life offers clues.

He was born in Virginia to a prosperous English merchant who sailed back to London while he was still a boy. His mother raised him in Roxbury, Massachusetts, then returned to England to rejoin her husband in the late 1660s. Burroughs stayed behind. He studied for the ministry at Harvard, graduating in 1670, a year after James Bayley, who would precede him in Salem Village as the town's first pastor. Another classmate, Samuel Sewall, would convict Burroughs for witchcraft two decades later.

Three years after his graduation, he married Hannah Fisher of Dedham, starting a family that in time would grow to nine children. Burroughs's grandfather had been a prominent English clergyman. Indeed, the ministry seemed to be in his blood. So when the people of Falmouth (now Portland, Maine) offered him two hundred acres to preach in the remote frontier outpost, he accepted.

He would stay two years. In 1676 King Philip's War brought death and ruin to the area, reducing the settlement to a smoking rash of razed homes, torched fields, and bloodied refugees. Burroughs helped evacuate the women and children to safety on Cushing's Island, subsisting on berries and fish until help arrived. He then followed the flood of evacuees down the coast to Massachusetts, where in November of 1680 he was offered a year's trial as Salem Village pastor. He must have passed muster, as he was offered the job the following year. In his acceptance agreement, perhaps anticipating what was to come, he stipulated that should a dispute arise between them, both sides must agree to mediation.

Now twenty-eight, he and his pregnant wife and two children moved in with John and Rebecca Putnam. It was cramped in their four-room home, an uncomfortable if temporary arrangement until a new parsonage could be built. Years later, Putnam would describe how "very good and dutiful" Hannah had been to him, though Burroughs was "very sharp" with her, making her sign and seal a statement promising not to divulge his "secrets" and, according to the Putnams, insisting on involving them in their personal disputes.

The Burroughses had already lost one child in infancy. When Hannah went into labor with their fourth, it killed her. The devastated pastor, caring for a newborn and two small children in an inhospitable household, now faced the added burden of a costly funeral. Since his salary wasn't due for another two months, John Putnam loaned him the money.

Before a year was out, Burroughs had remarried, this time to Sarah Ruck Hathorne of Salem, who would bear him four more children. Salem Village, meanwhile, was living up to its contentious reputation. Burroughs called meeting after meeting in a useless attempt to make peace. When he refused to call any more, Jeremiah Watts complained in a letter that rather than fostering Christian agreement, ministers only paid attention to their own preaching. Tired of the bickering and fed up with not being paid, Burroughs resigned. In the spring of 1683, he moved his family back to Falmouth, despite the threat of renewed Indian attacks, returning for the last time in April to settle accounts. The villagers had decided to deduct what Burroughs owed John Putnam for his wife's funeral from what they owed the pastor in unpaid wages. But in the first of several gross overreactions, Putnam had Burroughs arrested for debt. Six parishioners put up bail to prevent him from being taken to jail, but the damage was done: Burroughs's rapport with Salem Village was irreparably poisoned.

He returned to assist in Falmouth's reconstruction, though the impoverished settlers could barely scrape together enough to pay his salary. In 1689 Falmouth again fell under attack, yet remarkably, Burroughs survived. His second wife was less fortunate, probably dying from complications of childbirth. After shipping her remains back to Salem for burial, Burroughs moved south to Wells in 1690. Again he remarried, this time to a woman named Mary, who would bear him a daughter. By September of 1691, an attack seemed so imminent that many villagers had holed up in his garrison home, unable to bring in the harvest for fear of being killed. In the last letter penned from his book-lined study, Burroughs ruefully described the massacre that had destroyed York two days earlier, yet revealed no inclination to abandon Wells. Soon after, a group of helmeted men forced him to, charging their way into his home and interrupting his dinner.

Later court testimony brings Burroughs's Maine existence into focus. Besides preparing the weekly sermon, he schooled local boys, ministered to the sick and bereaved, and assisted selectmen with civic and military decisions. In short, he helped run the town. Felling trees, hauling provisions, raising barns, and plowing fields were all part of his routine. His skill in handling firearms suggests that he hunted game, and, by necessity, defended the village against Indian incursions. Commander Benjamin Church was so taken with his abilities that he promised to muster public funds to keep Burroughs on the Maine frontier.

Yet in 1692, these strengths were viewed with suspicion. Captain Simon Willard and Captain William Wormall were among the nine men who related stories of his prodigious feats. Though none had witnessed it, they had heard how he could single-handedly haul a barrel of cider or molasses onto shore from a rocking canoe, or lift an iron fowling piece with his index finger, though it had a seven-foot barrel. Burroughs denied it, explaining he had gripped the gun behind its lock and braced it against his chest. But his sheer presence had such a powerful affect on the afflicted girls that few doubted his guilt. Some fell limp to the floor; others were struck speechless, especially Mercy Lewis, who had lived in his household after her family was slain. So serious were the girls' fits that some had to be carried out of the room.

Asked what he made of the furor, Burroughs seemed baffled, saying only that he found it "an amazing and humbling Providence." Perhaps he blamed himself for keeping his first two wives on too short a leash. Despite his second wife's African slave girl and English maidservants, she probably lived in dread of an Indian attack, not to mention having to do without the creature comforts she had grown accustomed to in Salem. A Falmouth neighbor, Mary Webber, described Sarah Ruck Burroughs's dark forebodings. On one occasion, Sarah thought she saw Burroughs chase something resembling a white calf down the stairs. Another time, she had felt something invisible at her bedside, breathing on her. Too fearful of her husband to write a letter to her father, Webber had done it for her. Another former maidservant, Hannah Harris, related Burroughs's eerie ability to always know what his wife had said to her when the two women were alone together during the day. Sarah's brother, Thomas Ruck, told of a strawberry-picking expedition. When Burroughs disappeared into the bushes, leaving Sarah alone with her brother, she had used the opportunity to express her concerns. Suddenly Burroughs reappeared with a basket of berries, disputing Sarah's words. Surprised that Burroughs could have overheard the conversation, Thomas had asked him how he knew. "My god makes known your thoughts unto me," Burroughs ostensibly told him.

Judging by the tone of the interrogation, the minister's relations with his wives must have been a prime subject of gossip. Their ghosts had appeared to the afflicted girls, proclaiming that Burroughs had murdered them, along with the wife and child of Deodat Lawson. Harris, the former maidservant, complained that had he only let Sarah rest after she had given birth, instead of making her stand at the door while he railed on, perhaps she wouldn't have died. As it was, he neglected home prayer, she said, and baptized only one of his children, though records show that in fact four of his children had been baptized. Several witnesses testified that he was on a sinister quest to overthrow Salem Village. Burroughs protested several times, saying the witnesses were not being completely honest. He also handed the jury a letter in which he challenged the very existence of witches.

Though he proclaimed his innocence, his attempts at self-defense were oddly feeble. Reverend Increase Mather of Boston, who attended the trial, would later write that had he been one of the judges, "I could not have acquitted him."

Burroughs's August 19 execution drew a record number of spectators. A throng of prominent politicians and clergymen turned out to watch, even Cotton Mather, who rarely left Boston. George Burroughs's composure never faltered, from the moment they loaded him onto the back of the cart until he spoke his final words from the ladder. Together with four other condemned witches, he reiterated his innocence, persuaded Cotton Mather to pray with them, forgave others' sins and asked that his own be forgiven, and gave a flawless recitation of the Lord's Prayer.[2] That alone should have proved his innocence. Aware that real wizards were incapable of doing so, several emotional onlookers spoke out, questioning his guilt. But it was too late for such things. Reverend Cotton Mather calmed the crowd. Looking over them from atop his horse, he cautioned them not to be deceived. Remember, he said, that the devil himself "has often been transformed into an Angel of Light."

Those condemned to hang with him that day seemed at peace with their fate, possibly the effect of Burroughs's reassurance. Suddenly he was pushed off the ladder, his body swaying at the end of the rope. When his limbs ceased convulsing, the guards cut him down and removed his shirt and trousers, replacing them with those from a corpse. Then they heaved him into a common grave, burying him so hastily that at least one witness, Robert Calef, noticed that part of his chin and hand was left protruding from the soil.

MARTHA CARRIER, ANDOVER, 40s

One of the four prisoners who shared the gallows with George Burroughs that day was Martha Carrier, a farm wife with a keen sense of justice and a will of steel. Not only did she condemn the witchcraft charges, but actually told the judges off. Her defiance stunned the courtroom, leaving the magistrates more determined than ever to see her hang.

She was born into the family of Andrew and Faith Allen, one of twenty-two families that settled Andover in 1645 under the leadership of the colony's future governor, Simon Bradstreet. Her Scottish-born father built a farm in the southern part of the village near other Scots. As was customary, his plan was to bequeath his property—two house lots and several hundred acres—to his two sons, Andrew Jr. and John. Apart from Martha, who was born between them, the two boys were the youngest of his six children. Daughters Sarah and Hannah both married into the respectable Holt family, while his oldest, Mary, wed Roger Toothaker, a Billerica herbalist and physician. Martha moved in with the Toothakers while still a young teenager to help with the chores. It was in Billerica that she met Thomas Carrier, a Welsh immigrant several years her senior. They would marry in 1674, after she shocked the community by naming him the father of her child.

King Philip's War broke out the following year. Though living close to Indian territory, the Carriers did not abandon ship or seem to suffer terribly from the war's effects. Instead, their farm prospered. Only one other Billerica farm paid higher taxes. By the late 1680s, the Carrier family included three sons and a daughter, though an infant girl died only a few months old. But for reasons that remain unclear, their economic fortunes suffered an abrupt reversal. Now penniless, they returned to Andover, where Martha gave birth to their fifth child, a daughter. Fearing freeloaders, perhaps, the selectmen warned the family out, but soon had a change of heart and granted them land. The gesture was hardly a token of friendship. If anything, the community was losing patience with the struggling family. Strong-willed and articulate, Martha exhibited far too much independence for a woman of her station. When she and her children came down with smallpox in 1690, the selectmen quarantined the family and upbraided Martha for her "wicked carelessness," as if she had spread the disease on purpose.

She and her children recovered, but the contagion passed to her father, who died on Christmas day. It went on to kill both of her brothers, one of her brother's sons, and the husband and eldest son of her sister Hannah Holt. Another seven in the village would die that winter, for a total of thirteen. That the smallpox would bring down the men instead of the women, thus putting Martha's husband in line to inherit the Allen estate, made the villagers wonder if Martha hadn't sickened them by supernatural means. The suspicions festered until 1692, when Salem's afflicted girls glimpsed Martha's shape among the swirling specters.

She was the first witch suspect to be arrested from Andover. At her examination, Susannah Sheldon broke out of a trance to shout, "I wonder what could you murder 13 persons?" Mary Walcott saw a vision of thirteen ghosts, and Elizabeth Hubbard and Ann Putnam echoed the malevolent count. Martha accused them of lying, then turned and scolded the magistrates for believing the specious assertions of hysterical children. "It is a shamefull thing," she cried, "that you should mind these folks that are out of their wits."

Her boldness must have thrown the girls into a panic, as Reverend Samuel Parris wrote in his notes that "All the afflicted fell into most intolerable outcries & agonies." The shrieking reached such a deafening level that "there was no enduring of it." Guards had to be summoned to tie Martha's hands and feet and physically remove her from the room.

At her trial, a procession of former neighbors came forward to tell of cattle sickening and dying because of her malevolence. Andover neighbor Benjamin Abbot, who had engaged her family in property disputes, complained that her curses had caused sores to ooze on his foot, side, and groin, all of which healed once she was taken into custody. Her nephew Allen Toothaker was certain that she had aggravated his war wounds. But worst of all, four of her five children were arrested and compelled to testify against her. Torture loosened the tongues of her oldest sons, Richard and Andrew. The younger two, Thomas Jr., aged ten, and seven-year-old Sarah, readily confessed as if reading from a prepared script.

On August 19 Martha Carrier was loaded into the back of a cart with four convicted men and transported to Gallows Hill. She "died well," as one observer put it. Her children may have been forced to attend, so that the lesson would not be lost on them. When the noose had done its work, the guards removed her body from the scaffold and tossed it with the others in a rocky crevice. Cotton Mather, who watched it all from the saddle, would later note in his diary how surprised he was that this "rampant hag," who aspired to be "Queen of Hell," had dared to assert her innocence to the bitter end.

GILES COREY, SALEM, 70S

It was a losing proposition, no matter how you viewed it. Once accused, you bore the "witch" stigma for the rest of your days. Confess, and you languish in jail. Refuse to confess, and a rope chokes the life out of you. Either way, all your worldly goods are seized by the Crown.

For Giles Corey, that was not an option. He had worked many years to amass his estate, and it was an impressive one: three hundred acres in the southwest corner of Salem Village, today's Peabody. Having only had daughters, he would leave it to the two sons-in-law he could trust, William Cleeves and John Moulton, as the other two were not reliable. An inheritance, after all, was the only way to get ahead in life. So his mind was already made up in April of 1692, when he learned that his name had been linked with witchcraft. His wife, Martha, had been arrested the previous month, so it was hardly a surprise.

But then, he had more than his share of enemies. Though no devil, neither was Corey a saint. He was given to vile language and had filched a few things here and there, a bushel of apples, say, and yes, he could be quarrelsome. Folks got on his nerves. He had sued John Proctor, who'd had the gall to suggest that he'd set the Proctor house on fire. The suit was dropped when one of Proctor's own sons admitted to carelessness with a lamp. Even his own wife annoyed him. Martha was his third; in the two years since they'd married, she had driven him mad with her griping and gospelizing.

But the worst had been the Goodale incident. Almost seventeen years before, he had lost his temper and taken a stick to his dim-witted farmhand, Jacob Goodale. Martha and the boy's brother, Zachary, had brought the injured cretin to Dr. Endicott, but soon after, the fellow died. The autopsy found "clodders of blood about his heart," and a coroner's jury judged it murder. In the ensuing trial, several admitted to having thrashed the fellow, so Corey got off with a fine. Yet some in Salem Village couldn't forget it.

Now they'd get their vengeance. Essex County Marshal George Herrick came for him on April 18, and he was questioned the next day. Tight-lipped, he rebuffed their insinuations, while the Salem accusers mimicked his gestures and told their usual lies. He hardly knew what a warlock was, and now Abigail Hobbs was insisting he was one. Mercy Lewis called him "a dreadful wizard," dumping much of the same slander on him as they had on Martha the previous month. Then he was jailed to await his September arraignment. Until then, he would have to wait it out, hoping his sons-in-law would bring provisions.

At his September 9 arraignment, the grand jury heard more witnesses and read the indictments. He pleaded innocent, but when they asked him how he would be tried, expecting the usual "by God and my country," Corey dropped his little bomb. He remained silent. How surprised they looked. Indeed, he would be the first and only to "stand mute," as they termed it. The distinguished magistrates whispered to each other, frowning. They hadn't banked on this. Unsure what to do, they postponed the trial. Without this small utterance of consent, he was pleased to see, there couldn't be a trial. Perhaps they would test him, try to break his will. Certainly they would harangue him at the next session.

He hadn't anticipated the cruelty of their solution: *peine forte et dure,* a French term meaning pressing under stones. Such torture had been banned under Massachusetts law, but things were different now. English law had superseded the old charter. If he wouldn't submit of his own free will, they would crush it out of him.

On Monday, September 19, Sheriff George Corwin and six deputies took Corey from the jail and led him to an open field. He was stripped of his filthy clothes, and before several witnesses, forced to lie face up in a pit. They placed boards over him, then, one by one, started stacking heavy stones on top of him. With each new stone, they asked if he was ready to plead. Struggling to breathe under the weight, he made no sound. If they thought they could break him, they were sadly mistaken. He did not fear death—he was too old for that. Too old, too, to be cheated out of his estate.

After two days and nights of it, he was nearly done for. Several had tried to persuade him to change his mind, including a friend, Captain Thomas Gardner of Nantucket. A crowd stood around him now, observing his every labored breath. Three times Corwin asked whether he would submit to a trial, but Corey lacked the strength to speak. More stones were piled on, until the pressure got so great that his eyes bulged. Robert Calef noticed his tongue hanging limply out the side of his mouth and watched as Corwin pushed it in again with the tip of his cane.

The Salem Village church had excommunicated him the day before, and with difficulty, the guards had fed him three mouthfuls of bread and a few gulps of water. But on Monday, Corey could bear it no longer. At about noon, he drew his last breath. Legend has it that he cursed the town and its sheriff, but the most memorable were the two words that parted his lips: "More weight."

Just as Corey had anticipated, Sheriff Corwin turned up at the farm, claiming he would confiscate their property for the Crown unless a fine was promptly paid. He was lying, but Corey's son-in-law John Moulton sold some livestock at a loss and paid Corwin off. Giles Corey lost his life, but not his estate; it remained in the family.

MARTHA COREY, SALEM, 70s?

For years she had harbored a shameful secret. Giles Corey had married her nonetheless, but the aging farmer turned out to be mean and uncouth. It wasn't beyond him to announce that what he knew about her would "fix her business" if ever it got out. So she felt blessed when in 1690, the year they wed, she was accepted into the Salem Village church as a full member. She felt redeemed, as if her sins had been forgiven. She resolved to live up to her new status, correcting her husband's behavior when necessary, and conducting herself as befitted one of the elect.

No mention of her past is found in the Salem witch trial transcripts. Yet it is unlikely that such gossip would have escaped the ears of her neighbors, especially revelations that in 1677 Martha Corey had given birth to a mulatto son named Ben, and spent ten years raising him in a Salem boardinghouse while her husband, Henry Rich, raised their white son, Thomas. But perhaps being the wife of a murderer was reason enough to knock Martha Corey down a peg. Her holier-than-thou attitude certainly couldn't have helped.

Her fall from grace began in early March. The first witch suspects were to be questioned at Ingersoll's Tavern, and Giles decided to go. Disgusted, Martha criticized him for wanting to watch such nonsense and flung the saddle off his horse. He went anyway, telling others of her outburst. Then on March 12, two church deacons, Edward Putnam and Ezekiel Cheever, rode out to inform Martha that her specter had been seen. They stopped first at Thomas Putnam's house to ask his afflicted daughter, Ann Jr., how the apparition had been dressed. But the child's preternatural vision was obstructed that day, so the deacons continued on. They found Martha alone, smiling uncomfortably.

"I know what you are come for," she said sweetly. "You are come to talk with me about being a witch, but I am none. I cannot help people's talking of me."

Putnam acknowledged that Ann Jr. had named her.

"But does she tell you what clothes I have on?" The men did not respond, so she repeated the question. When they admitted to Ann's temporary blindness, Martha smiled again, seemingly unperturbed. Nor did she seem upset when they cautioned that spectral sightings such as hers reflected poorly on the congregation. She expressed no mercy for the arrested, calling them "idle slothful persons" who "minded nothing that was good." She, on the other hand, embraced Christ, she insisted, and rejoiced at the Word of God.

Circumstances worsened for Martha on March 20, when Abigail Williams pointed her finger to the ceiling of the meetinghouse, interrupting the Sunday service. Martha Corey's specter, she exclaimed, was sitting on a beam up there with her yellow bird. Her neighbors hushed her, but Abigail ignored them, tracing the phantom bird's flight to the pulpit, and from there to Reverend Deodat Lawson's hat on its peg. Martha watched the little drama in silence. But early the next morning, Constable Joseph Herrick picked her up and brought her in to Ingersoll's Tavern for questioning.

The afflicted group had grown, and the inn was so full that they moved the examination over to the meetinghouse. When Martha walked in, the girls collapsed into screaming fits. Judge Hathorne turned to Martha for an explanation.

"Pray give me leave to go to prayer," she replied. She prayed aloud until he intervened: "We do not send for you to go to prayer," he barked. Again he asked why she was attacking the children.

"I am an innocent person," she replied. "I never had to do with witchcraft since I was born. I am a Gospel Woman."

"Do not you see these complain of you?" he said, referring to the suffering girls.

"The Lord open the eyes of the magistrates and ministers," Martha preached. "The Lord show His power to discover the guilty."

Despite Martha's pleas of innocence, the accusations increased. Then her husband's oxen seemed unable to rise from their hind quarters, and his cat seemed close to death, making him wonder if there wasn't something to the suspicions. Martha suggested giving the cat's head a knock, but he refused.

After her conviction September 10, the church voted to excommunicate her, so a committee of church dignitaries paid her a visit at Salem prison. Reverend Samuel Parris accompanied them, writing later that "we found [her] very obdurate," justifying herself and "condemning all that had done anything to her just discovery or condemnation." She lectured them and refused (for once) to join them in prayer. Then they broke the news.

She was hanged September 22, but not before proclaiming her innocence and reciting a lengthy prayer. Perhaps it pleased her to know that she had outlived her husband, who had been pressed to death three days earlier. But she would never have the gratification of learning that the church would realize its mistake and restore her membership, sins or no sins, in 1703.

LYDIA DUSTIN, READING, 79

Though a full-standing member of the church, she could be disagreeable. It wasn't so much her peppery speech as her bent-over shape that stirred speculation that Lydia Dustin might be in league with the devil. A few years before, a local drunkard had pitched stones at her daughter's home, railing out loud about that "old crooked-back witch, your mother, you, and all your company of witches."

Then in May of 1692, as Salem grappled with revelations of witchcraft, a Malden neighbor, Mary Marshall, came forward with a shocking disclosure. Four local women, she declared, had colluded with Satan to harm her: Widow Dustin and her married daughter, Mary Coleson, as well as Mary Taylor and Widow Lilley. Marshall was feeling particularly susceptible, as her second husband, Edward, had just died.

The day the four were arrested, Widow Marshall began suffering physical afflictions that would last several months, torments she blamed on Mary Coleson. The woman's specter, she claimed, was avenging the arrest of her mother.

Another of Lydia's daughters, Sarah, who was in her thirties yet still unmarried, was arrested the same month.

Upon further questioning, Marshall disclosed that a few days earlier, the three younger women had dropped by with the news that the minister, Reverend Pierpont, had sung a psalm containing the words, "God will be a husband to the widow." But instead of using the news to comfort the grieving widow, the three hissed that God "would be none to her" and that had she served Him, her husband would still be alive.

At Lydia Dustin's trial in September, she was told to turn and face Mary Marshall and her other accusers. Predictably, they fell convulsing to the floor, and when Lydia touched them, their symptoms disappeared. She denied the charges against her, yet said little in her own defense, apart from reminding the court that God would not condone the harsh treatment of a widow. As far as the justices were concerned, Lydia Dustin had just proven her satanic powers; she might even have played a role, they thought, in Edward Marshall's death.

At her Charlestown indictment in February of 1693, a large crowd gathered to hear her enter a plea of not guilty. At least thirty witnesses regaled the judges with tales of her quarrels and the spectral misdeeds that had ensued. Yet despite all the evidence, the jury found her not guilty. She was free to go.

Free—once her jail fees were paid. But Lydia Dustin lacked the money, so back to her cell she went. Four weeks later, still unable to come up with the money, she died in Cambridge prison.

MARY EASTY, TOPSFIELD, 56

After her death, Boston merchant Robert Calef would praise Mary Easty as a person "as Serious, Religious, Distinct, and Affectionate as could well be exprest." But even before her execution, over a hundred of her neighbors and relatives had signed a petition attesting to her sterling character, all to no avail.

She was doomed. For one thing, two of her older sisters, Rebecca Nurse and Sarah Cloyce, had already been pulled into the vortex; though Sarah survived, all three were frequently reminded that their mother, Johanna Towne, had been a witch before them. Mary's older sister Rebecca had been the first arrested. While she suffered in jail, her sisters worked tirelessly on her behalf, taking petitions around for their frightened neighbors to sign. Perhaps the women's determination was what made the justices turn on them.

Most of the eight Towne siblings lived close to one another. Mary had wed Isaac Easty thirty-seven years before and lived with him on a Topsfield farm. They had eight boys and four girls. The youngest, Jeffrey, was twelve.

Since March, when the constable had come for Rebecca, Mary probably lived in dread that she would be next, and indeed, they came for her in April. At her questioning, the Salem girls mimicked her every gesture. When Mary lowered her head, they screamed that she was trying to break their necks. Mercy Lewis claimed that Easty's specter had gotten into her bed and put her hand on her breasts, which seemed to clinch it for Judge Hathorne.

Mary insisted she was innocent. "Sir, I never complyed but prayed against him all my dayes, I have no complyance with Satan, in this. . . . I am clear of this sin."

Then what could be causing these sufferings, he asked. "It is an evil spirit," she replied, "but whither it be witchcraft I do not know."

Hathorne's response was thick with sarcasm. "Marvelous" that she would not think them bewitched, considering the fact that several had already confessed to being witches. With that final remark, he ordered her to jail.

After languishing for a month on the filthy dirt floor of Salem prison, she was re-examined on May 18, but this time, the afflicted girls seemed uncertain of her guilt. Only Mercy Lewis insisted that Mary's specter had attacked her. Seeing no reason to keep her, the justices released the exhausted woman into her family's custody. But her specter returned to accost the girls, so she was re-arrested two days later.

By the time of her September 9 trial, Mary Easty was prepared.

Eight men testified to the great suffering that Mercy Lewis had endured, and two witnesses described Mary's witchcraft. For her part, she produced statements from Ipswich and Boston jailers attesting to her good behavior, and called her children, her minister, and members of her church as character witnesses. She urged the judges to advise her and not to place too much importance on spectral evidence, stories about the supposed doings of her specter, considering that she had "for many yeares Lived under the unblemished reputation of Christianity."

They condemned her nonetheless. In a frank and movingly worded petition addressed to Governor William Phipps, the pastors, and the judges, she made a last effort to instill reason into the proceedings. She asked not that her own life be saved, despite her innocence and the "wiles" of her accusers, but that "no more Innocentt blood may be shed." She knew the justices "would not be guilty of Innocent blood for the world," but cautioned them to "strictly" question the accusers and keep them separated for a while. They should also take more care in trying the confessed witches, as several had lied.

On September 22, she and seven others, all but one of them women, were loaded into the back of an oxcart for the trip to Gallows Hill. A crowd straggled behind. As the cart turned up the hill, its wheels stuck. Some of the accusers started to shriek, crying that the devil was holding it back, but a group of men managed to push it out.

From her rung on the ladder, the noose around her neck and her hands and skirts bound with rope, Mary Easty prayed for an end to the witch hunt. Boston merchant Robert Calef, who witnessed the executions, would write that she so movingly bade farewell to her husband and family that it drew "tears from the Eyes of almost all present." The executioner seems to have been less moved, as he pushed her off the ladder, leaving her to choke to death from the force of her own weight.

ANN FOSTER, ANDOVER, 70S

Though by no means the oldest defendant, she was so frail that they had to carry her into the courtroom. It was a bitter reckoning for Widow Foster, who with her husband, Andrew, had been among the first freeholders to set down roots in Andover's south end. They had wanted to live near fellow Scots Robert Russell and Andrew Allen, and they had worked hard.

But after her husband's death in 1685, a pall seemed to hang over the Foster household. As was customary in those days, Andrew bequeathed the property to their two sons. She was left with a few head of livestock, supplies of grain and firewood, and use of the family home. Grieving, they had carried on.[3]

Then in 1689, Ann's son-in-law got into a drunken rage. While out walking one evening with his wife, he had slit her throat, though she was eight months pregnant. Andover's first murder couldn't have been more senseless. Hugh and Hannah Stone had been married twenty-two years; it would have been their eighth child.[4]

At his execution the following year, Reverend Thomas Barnard asked Stone what had possessed him. He blamed the family, saying they had been contentious and that his wife had not obeyed him. In his final words from the gallows, he urged the men in the crowd to honor their marriage vows, and their wives to know their place. Then, to Ann's horror, he viciously rebuked her.

The same year, his orphaned son Simon had traveled to Exeter, New Hampshire, where he was ambushed by Indians. Warriors shot him in nine places and axed him twice in the neck, attempting to cut off his head. When English soldiers appeared in the distance, the attackers fled. Simon, lying unconscious among the dead, was assumed slain until a soldier heard him gasp. Miraculously, they nursed him back to health. It would take longer for the family to outlive the stigma of Hannah's murder, if they ever could.

When Salem fell to witches two years later, Ann was among the first to be arrested. Perhaps the villagers couldn't rid their thoughts of Hugh Stone's final words. Feeble, sick, and lacking friends who might assist her, Ann surrendered to the uproar without a struggle. Blaming herself, perhaps, for her family's trials, she confessed to virtually every charge. Yes, she had bewitched John Lovejoy's hog. Yes, she had infected Andrew Allen's son with the smallpox, and another child, too, and hurt Timothy Swan. The only thing she denied was her daughter's and granddaughters' claim that they were witches, too.

The court found her guilty, but Ann Foster would be spared the gallows. Heartsick and depleted after five months in shackles, she died in her prison cell. Her son Abraham would have to pay two pounds and ten shillings to retrieve her corpse.

SARAH GOOD, SALEM VILLAGE, 38

She was ragged and filthy, a foul-smelling, pipe-smoking annoyance who roamed Salem Village with her five-year-old daughter, begging. To look at her was to feel pity, yet those who offered charity were thanked with scowls and curses, as if accepting handouts was somehow beneath her. Many gave her gifts of food to make her go away. In a society that viewed wealth as a sign of God's blessing, Sarah Good must have seemed like so much human refuse, blaming all and sundry for her own failings. Yet Sarah was only partly to blame for her dismal situation.

She was raised in Wenham, a town just northeast of Salem Village, one of seven children born to a well-heeled innkeeper of French heritage named John Soulart. In 1672, when she was eighteen, her father drowned, though town records, which refer to him as "the Frenchman," ruled it a suicide. Her mother soon remarried, and the majority of Soulart's extensive estate, including five hundred pounds sterling and seventy-seven acres, was snapped up by Sarah's stepfather.

Sarah and her siblings sued yet were unable to extract their shares. So in 1682 they approached the Massachusetts General Court. Sarah argued that she deserved more than the mere three acres of meadow she had been granted. The court concurred, and she received a small plot of land.

But it was only the beginning of Sarah's woes. She had married Daniel Poole, who ordered a fine suit of clothing for himself and two dresses for Sarah, then unexpectedly died, leaving her saddled with a seven-pound debt. Funeral expenses set her back even more. To pay them, she sold her horse, two cows, and most of her belongings. A year later, she married William Good, a weaver. By this time, her stepfather had agreed to let her have a meadow, but Poole's creditors pursued her. She was given no choice but to sell part of her hard-won land. By the end of the summer, she had sold it all.

Eventually she and her husband were reduced to begging. In the days before poor farms and welfare, the indigent relied on the mercy of neighbors. To evade such burdens, seventeenth-century selectmen "warned out" individuals of questionable income, alerting them that they would receive no handouts should they fall on hard times. Whether Salem Village warned out Sarah and William Good is not clear, but the homeless couple must have proved an embarrassment to more fortunate families, especially those who were disinclined to help. Mortified at having fallen so low, Sarah could be vindictive, muttering curses at offerings that fell short of her expectations.

To some, witchcraft offered a plausible explanation for Sarah's eccentric behavior, especially when her own husband suggested as much. Court documents reflect the degree of their mutual recriminations. A day after Sarah's April 30 arrest, William told officials he "was afraid that she either was a witch or would be one very quickly." Asked why he thought this, he explained that she behaved badly toward him and, perhaps in an unintended pun, was "an enemy to all good." On March 5, William Good told the magistrates that the night before Sarah's interrogation, he had noticed "a wart or tit a little below her right shoulder" that he had never seen before. This damning statement was all the evidence her detractors needed. Sarah must be guilty. Why else would she have grown a witch's tit to suckle the devil's familiars?

But even without William's lies, the village must have welcomed a chance to have it out about her. Samuel and Mary Abbey had opened their home to the piteous couple, only to turn them out again, they explained, when Sarah's tirades became too much to bear. Henry Herrick recalled the time she had stopped by his father's farm begging for a place to sleep. His father had refused, instructing him to escort her off the property and make sure she didn't hide in the barn, where her pipe might start a fire. Sarah and Thomas Gadge spurned her request for food and clothing, fearing she might infect them with smallpox.

At her trial, Sarah's five-year-old, Dorothy, was quickly manipulated into substantiating that her mother was a witch. The child had been placed in her father's care after her mother's incarceration, but in March, even she was arrested for witchcraft.

Judge Hathorne treated the homeless woman with contempt. Sarah wasn't beyond casting blame on others but denied any guilt of her own, often in a fit of temper.

Covered as she was in layers of stinking skirts, no one noticed that she was pregnant. After her conviction, she and Dorothy were sent to Boston, as the Salem jail was full. It was there that Sarah gave birth. Governor Simon Bradstreet ordered the jail-keeper to provide her with two blankets at a cost of ten shillings, but in the clammy darkness, the infant arrived stillborn.

On July 19, after four and a half months, prison guards separated her from five-year-old Dorothy and transported her to Salem Village for her execution. A noose was thrown over her neck, and those of five others. Their hands were tied, and they were forced up ladders. When it came her turn, Reverend Nicholas Noyes urged her for the final time to confess, as "she was a witch, and she knew she was a witch."

But Sarah got the last jab, calling him a liar. "I am no more a Witch than you are a Wizard," she said, "and if you take away my Life, God will give you Blood to drink."

Eighteen years later, after Massachusetts had realized that the witch trials had all been a horrible mistake, William Good applied to the authorities for restitution. Though remarried, he was still taking handouts. Dorothy had survived her months alone in Boston jail, though not without psychological injury. In his request, Good cited Dorothy's rough treatment. The experience had so terrified her that ever since then, he said, she had been "very chargeable, having little or no reason to govern herself."

Elizabeth Howe, Topsfield, 50s

The cloud of gossip started with the Perleys' sick daughter. Unable to diagnose her prickling sensations, a doctor had declared her the victim of "an evil hand." Within a few years, the ten-year-old had "pined away to skin and bones" and died. From that day forward, Elizabeth Howe could not seem to shake the stigma that she was a witch.

The stories were so malicious that she feared they would ruin her chances of becoming a member in the Ipswich church. To seek support, she paid a visit to the wife of Joseph Stafford. "I believe you are not ignorant," Howe confided, taking the woman's hand, "of the great Scandal that I lye under by an evil Report raised upon me." Stafford acted sympathetic, but she would later depose that she was too frightened of Howe to refuse her request. So at the next church meeting, she supported Howe's acceptance into church membership "like one Enchanted," singing the woman's praises for two or three hours, even though Samuel Perley and Isaac Foster had already nixed it.

Then suddenly Goody Stafford fell into a trance. When she came to, she cried, "Ha! I was mistaken!" Asked what she meant, Stafford said, "I thought Goody Howe had been a precious Saint of God, but now I see she is a Witch: She has bewitched me, and my Child, and we shall never be well, till there be a Testimony for her that she may be taken into the Church." Howe was sorry to learn of Goody Stafford's troubles, but her empathy mattered little. As far as Stafford was concerned, Howe had deceived her, and her evil apparition was penetrating the clapboards.

After that, every little misfortune was laid at Elizabeth's feet. Samuel Perley accused her of driving his cow mad and making it drown in a pond. Goodwife Sherwin, with whom Elizabeth had quarreled, fell sick and died, raving that Elizabeth had bewitched her. Several who had fallings-out with her unaccountably found their cider and beer spoiled or spilled from the barrels. Martha Wood suffered a strange amnesia after eating an apple that Elizabeth had given her, and Isaac Cummings had trouble with his mare. Having refused to lend it to Elizabeth's husband, Cummings found the animal abused, "as if burnt with a red hot Bridle." Assuming that witches had used it for a joy ride, he and his brother-in-law, Thomas Andrews, attempted various cures, but none of them worked. Andrews took a pipe of burning tobacco and inserted it into the horse's rectum. It burned with a blue flame, covering the mare's rump and flaring up to the barn's rafters. The next day being the Sabbath, Cummings let the mare be, as he needed to ride it to the service. That night his neighbor, John Hunkins, suggested that cutting off and burning a piece of the horse's flesh might prove beneficial. Cummings thought he'd try it the next day, but as they walked from the barn, the mare fell dead.

Distracted by their personal grievances, few of the villagers took notice of Elizabeth's dire situation. Her husband, James, whom she had married at twenty-three, had gone blind seven years earlier. Their six children helped with the chores, but she shouldered the burden of running the farm and caring for him. Being related by marriage to the Reverend Francis Dane of Andover, she would be scapegoated, as were virtually all of the women in Dane's family, by Salem's bewitched girls. She was also the subject of envy, being in line to inherit a third of her father's substantial estate.

She would never live to see the property, as she was arrested that May. She could not bring herself to confess, saying, "If it was the last moment I was to live, God knows I am innocent of anything in this nature." At her trial a month later, at least twelve neighbors attested to her innocence, including her husband's ninety-four-year-old father, who described her as "very dutiful, careful, loving, obedient, and kind, tenderly leading her husband about by the hand in his want of eyesight." Even Reverend Samuel Phillips and Reverend Payson of Rowley described personally hearing Timothy Perley's daughter ensure Elizabeth that she had done nothing to cause the girl's illness. On the same visit, they heard the girl's brother urge his sister, "Say Goodwife Howe is a witch, say she is a witch!"

Yet their protestations fell on deaf ears. Instead, the jury focused on the litany of Topsfield neighbors who traced their dead farm animals and spoiled cider to Elizabeth's wickedness. She was executed at Gallows Hill on July 19 with her sister-in-law, Rebecca Nurse, and three other women. Thereafter, her daughters Mary and Abigail Howe told of their father's twice-weekly journeys to Boston. For the duration of Elizabeth's month-long incarceration, he had brought her food, drink, and clean linen, "which was provided with much difficulty." One of the two girls always went with him, they said, "because he could not go alone for want of sight."

GEORGE JACOBS SR., SALEM, 80s

Toothless and lame, with a ragged beard and limbs deformed by arthritis, the elderly George Jacobs moved slowly, propelling himself on his two wooden canes. Yet for all his infirmities, he was as sharp as the magistrates and, though usually well mannered, was known to have used his cane on his twenty-year-old maidservant, Sarah Churchill.

Perhaps he used it once too often. Sarah's complaints of his mistreatment would land him in a scorching jail until his execution for witchcraft, and though he had lived a full life, it was not how he wanted to die. The afflicted girls repeated Sarah's unthinking words until the magistrates seemed convinced of his guilt, yet the old man, incredulous at their gullibility, confronted them.

"Your worships. All of you. Do you think this is true?"

They only threw the question back at him, so he asked Sarah Churchill to prove his guilt. When she described how his specter had accosted her at Ingersoll's Tavern, and how Mary Warren had known it was him as she had seen his two canes, he fell down on his knees before the judges.

"Pray, do not accuse me," he begged. "I am as clear as your worships. You must do right judgments."

But the magistrates sided with Sarah, turning his pleas into rage. "You tax me for a wizard," he hissed. "You may as well tax me for a buzzard! I have done no harm!"

Sarah begged to differ, saying she knew he had led "a wicked life." She never followed her claims up with facts, but she didn't have to. His neighbors knew that George Jacobs Sr. had worked thirty-three years to make his farm prosperous. Having outlived his first wife, he was living with his second, Mary Jacobs, and with his granddaughter Margaret. His property, Northfields, was located about halfway between Salem Village and Salem.

Being outspoken, he had belittled the afflicted girls early on. In March he had even disrupted a Salem lecture that had been called to pray for them.

The fact that he had dictated a will that January suggests that his mortality was ever present in his thoughts. It also holds clues to his family: Though small, it seemed close-knit. The house would go to his wife. Upon her death, it would pass to their son George, then to their grandson, another George. Should they die, it would pass to his daughter and her husband, Ann and John Andrews, a Salem shipwright. The grandchildren would receive the household goods, and Margaret, who was seventeen, would get a milking cow and certain items from the gun room. At least that was the plan. But everything changed in early May, when Margaret saw a vision of Alice Parker, a Salem widow.

Jacobs was interrogated five days later. It did not go well, and they questioned him again the next day. This time, Ann Putnam Jr. involved his granddaughter Margaret in her spurious charges. Jacobs denied all, but the girls garnered the crowd's sympathy when pins were discovered jabbing their hands. Margaret was then brought up before the magistrates. The afflicted girls, noting that her visions had ceased, concluded that she too had joined the witches. In her terror, the girl caved in, confessing her grandfather's guilt.

In Salem jail, he was strip-searched for witches' marks. They discovered a quarter-inch growth on his right shoulder and lanced it with a sharp object, but nothing came out. Later, a seven-man team searched him again, this time finding moles on his right hip, his back, and inside his right cheek. Yet despite the privations, he got a scribe to make changes in his will. His wife would still get the house, but only until she remarried. Then it would pass not to their son George, who had fled to parts unknown, but to George's fifteen-year-old son, whose unbalanced mother, Rebecca, had been left alone to care for their five young children. When Constable Jonathan Putnam had arrested her, she had left them unattended, running after the cart crying, until the horse sped up and their forms were overtaken by distance. Jacobs crossed Ann and John Andrews out completely, as they had turned their backs on him. But he inserted ten pounds silver for Margaret, who had found the courage to pull herself together and tell the truth, albeit in vain.

Sheriff George Corwin meanwhile had ridden out to the farm and seized over seventy-nine pounds worth of his property: five cows, five swine, a mare, various fowl, eight loads of hay, sixty bushels of corn, and apples enough to make a dozen barrels of cider. They scoured the house, making off with coins, a gold thumb ring, all the bedding, and two brass kettles, along with furniture and pewter. They confiscated Mary's wedding ring, though she would eventually win it back, and even stripped the pantry, leaving her so destitute that she was forced to buy back some of her own foodstuffs. Some of the neighbors—but few relatives—offered help.

On August 19, George Jacobs Sr. was taken to Gallows Hill with five other convicted witches, Samuel Wardwell, John Proctor, John Willard, Martha Carrier, and Reverend George Burroughs. He never confessed.

By February of the following year, his son George Jacobs Jr. was still in hiding, so his brother-in-law, John Andrews, went alone to the Essex County probate court to settle the will. The court had both versions but ignored the amended one, which had left the Andrewses out. By June, George Jacobs Jr. had returned home and taken over the farm, against his late father's wishes.

The same month, his widow, Mary, remarried, just as Jacobs had anticipated. But her choice of husbands might have surprised the old man. He was John Wildes, whose own wife, Sarah, had been hanged for witchcraft.

As for Jacobs himself, a family member, perhaps his teenage grandson, may have recovered his body and transported it home for reburial, because two centuries later, a grave was found on what had been Jacobs's farm. The remains were those of an old, toothless man.[5]

Susannah Martin, Amesbury, 71

There's no way to tell what started the gossip. Perhaps it was her bluntness. For thirty years, infamous stories about Susannah Martin's malefic crimes had accumulated until Salem authorities hanged her for witchcraft on July 19. She was so hardened to it all by 1692 that when her youthful accusers fell convulsing to the meetinghouse floor, she just laughed.

"What?" asked the stunned magistrate. "Do you laugh at it?"

"Well I may laugh at such folly."

"Is this folly, the hurt of these persons?"

"I never hurt man, woman, or child!"

Her blistering contempt at the proceedings could hardly have helped her case. She belittled her accusers, addressing one as "sweetheart" and denying that they were bewitched. Ann Putnam Jr. became so incensed that she threw her glove at the woman. Yet however vindictive she became, she would remain true to herself on one point: She would not tell a lie, even "if it would save my life."

What little survives about her life suggests a troubled existence. Susannah North was born in England, the youngest of three daughters whose mother died young. Her father remarried, then moved the family to New England, settling in Salisbury, Massachusetts. In 1646, at twenty-five, Susannah married George Martin, a local widower. One of their nine children would die in infancy. But her impetuous nature was already showing itself by 1648, when she was fined twenty shillings for an unspecified offense. Twenty years later, the village would demonstrate its disregard for her by seating her near the back of the meetinghouse.

But an even greater blow followed her father's death in 1668. Since she and her sister, Mary Jones, were the only surviving children, they expected to divide his one-hundred-fifty-pound estate soon after his demise, or at least after the passing of his wife, Ursula North. But to their surprise, the old will had been replaced with a new one, which despite dubious errors left virtually everything to their stepmother. Susannah, her sister, and a niece, Ann Bates, were left with a paltry twenty-two pounds.

After that, her standing in the village seemed to suffer. William and Thomas Sargent started a rumor that she was a witch, and that before she married, she had given birth to an illegitimate child and strangled it. Her husband sued William for slander and won, but the court acquitted him on the witchcraft. Susannah was then summoned to court on charges of witchcraft. She was probably acquitted, but the gossip didn't stop. She appeared in court again that fall, this time for calling her neighbor a liar and thief. The defamation must have taken its toll on the whole family. Susannah's son Richard, who they had called her imp, also left a mark in the record books for pushing his father down, stripping him, and threatening him with an axe.

Then in 1671, Susannah's stepmother died, leaving the estate to her granddaughter, Mary Winsley, and her child, Hepzibah. Disinherited, Susannah and her sister contested the will. Several witnesses spoke in their defense, but the court was not convinced. The family would appeal the ruling numerous times, all to no avail. So by 1692, when Salem's afflicted girls were clamoring for more victims, Susannah was prime fodder.

Even though she proclaimed her innocence, the jury had plenty of evidence. At least nine of her neighbors had made the trip to Salem to relate the damage she had done them over the years, from drowning their oxen to flinging cats through second-story windows to gnaw at their throats. When the judge suggested that God and indeed the whole congregation thought her guilty, she only scoffed at them:

"Let them think what they will."

REBECCA NURSE, SALEM VILLAGE, 71

She was a selfless nurturer, a devout farm wife and loving mother who took in a foster child on top of raising eight of her own. Of all those charged, she might have been the most saintly. Yet she was not only forced from her sickbed to answer charges of witchcraft, but strip-searched, excommunicated, and finally hanged, though thirty-nine of her neighbors, friends, and fellow church members signed petitions in her defense. Ultimately, Rebecca Nurse became the victim of misplaced envy.

Born in England in 1621, Rebecca Towne immigrated as a young girl to Massachusetts with her parents and seven siblings. The Townes built a modest farm in Topsfield, just north of Salem. Her father struggled with the usual property disputes over the years, and some suspected that her mother, Johannah Towne, might be a witch. Since diabolical powers were believed to be inherited, the gossip would come back to haunt Rebecca later.

In the 1640s, she married Francis Nurse, a woodworker, and moved to a farm in Salem. They were solid and responsible. Francis did jury and constable duty. Then in 1678, they acquired the impressive Salem Village estate of a Boston clergyman, James Allen. It looked as if the Nurses had come into a windfall, but in fact they had negotiated a lease-to-buy arrangement on the three-hundred-acre property. The plan was that they would work hard and use the profits from the farm to buy the property when the lease expired in twenty-one years. Still, the Nurses' impressive new homestead inspired envy, and with good reason. They made every payment on time, and their diligence was turning profits. In 1690 Francis Nurse's tax rate rose by 39 percent over 1681. Though they lived closer to Salem, Rebecca opted to become a member of the struggling Salem Village church, even though her husband and father had a history of boundary disputes with the Putnams, who also attended. Perhaps her overriding goal was to set a good example for her children, all eight of whom settled nearby.

Then in March of 1692, twelve-year-old Ann Putnam Jr. saw Rebecca's apparition, and this most devout and good-hearted of women became the sixth charged that year with witchcraft. Now seventy-one, years of toil had left her ill and hard of hearing. According to court testimony, she told visitors that she had heard about the girls' afflictions and regretted that she wasn't well enough to visit them, but had prayed for them. Informed that her own name had been linked to witchcraft, she wondered aloud what sin she could have committed that God "should lay such an affliction on me in my old age."

Too weary to confront her accusers, Rebecca simply told the truth: She was "innocent as the child unborn." Called before the magistrates to hear Ann Putnam Jr.'s hateful charges, she stood unsteadily before the packed meetinghouse, saying only, "Oh Lord help me." The girls mimicked her gestures in demonstration of her alleged sorcery, yet instead of scolding them, Rebecca expressed bafflement and despair. The usual band of accusers went through the by now familiar physical torments to "prove" Rebecca's guilt. A group of local goodwives stripped and searched her, uncovering a "supernatural mark" on her genitalia. Try as she might to explain that it was a childbirth-related scar, her explanation was ignored.

In early June a grand jury deliberated her case. To the delight of her friends and neighbors, she was found not guilty. But the afflicted girls made such a hue and cry that the judges reconsidered, calling Rebecca back for further questioning. One answer in particular seemed suspicious. Asked if she had worked in league with another accused witch, Rebecca had referred to the woman in earlier testimony as "one of our company." Asked now to explain what she meant by that remark, Rebecca merely gazed up at the judges with a confused look. Later it came to light that being hard of hearing, she had not heard the question.

But the judges interpreted her silence as an admission of guilt and sentenced her to death. Her supporters pressed for her release, going so far as to persuade the governor, Sir William Phips, to order a reprieve. But again the afflicted girls cried foul, and Phips backed down. The most vociferous were the Putnams, signing ten of the eighteen depositions sworn against her. It wasn't so much Rebecca they scorned as what she represented, namely the prosperity and community esteem that seemed to elude them.

Rebecca Nurse was hanged on July 19, her body heaved into a shallow grave in a rocky cleft. An enduring legend maintains that her family stole her body away under cover of darkness and reburied her on the farm, in a spot marked today with a fine headstone. Her homestead, as handsome and well-tended as she would have kept it, is now a museum.

Sarah Osborne, Salem Village, 40s

Many would say she had it coming. For years she had lived under a cloud of disapproval. When rumors of witchcraft started spreading in 1692, Sarah Osborne's name sprung instantly to people's lips. She had long been ill, and according to some, her husband beat her. But her worst sin, perhaps, was greed.

She had begun life as Sarah Warren in Watertown, Massachusetts. In 1662 she married Robert Prince, who had purchased a one-hundred-and-fifty-acre farm in Salem. His sister was married to Captain John Putnam, who lived next door. Putnam was part of a faction that supported Salem Village's new parson, Samuel Parris, and the village's independence from Salem. Prince died in 1674, leaving his land in trust to Sarah, on the understanding that she would divide it between their two sons, James and Joseph, when they came of age. As executors, Prince had named his two brothers-in-law, John and Thomas Putnam.

Now widowed with two small children, Sarah sought help tending the farm. She found a young Irishman, Alexander Osborne, purchasing his indenture for fifteen pounds sterling. Though considerably older than he, the two became romantically involved. Eventually they married, but the notion of an unmarried man and woman sharing the same roof—even temporarily—had set tongues to wagging. An even bigger scandal was looming.

Sarah, perhaps anticipating more children, decided to challenge her late husband's will and fight for control of his property.[6]

The legal battle lasted years. Before it was resolved, Sarah and Alexander Osborne were long dead, and her sons were fifty-two and forty-eight. But the Putnams' revenge was as swift as the court proceedings were slow.

In February of 1692, Thomas Putnam, his brother Edward, and two others rode to Salem to file complaints against Sarah Osborne, Sarah Good, and Tituba for wreaking "mischief" against Ann Putnam Jr. and three local girls. Though she had been bedridden for more than a year, Sarah was arrested the following day and carted to Salem Village for questioning.

On May 10, as the witch hunt was just taking off, Sarah Osborne became its first victim, her heart giving out in the jail's gloom. Frail even before enduring the difficult voyage to Boston, she had lain in the cold for nine weeks and two days. Jail keeper John Arnold made a note of the number of days in jail in his ledger, adding that her prison bill—one pound and three shillings—had been left unpaid.

ALICE PARKER, SALEM, AGE UNKNOWN

Her name came up, almost as an afterthought, in the questioning of Mary Warren, John Proctor's troubled maidservant. The magistrates, having succeeded in wringing noxious stories from the girl about Proctor, pressed her for more. Not wishing to disappoint them, she disclosed that the phantoms of two local women, Alice Parker and Ann Pudeator, had brought her rag dolls resembling two of her fellow sufferers, Mercy Lewis and Mary Walcott, and that she had jabbed the dolls with pins. She named a few other likely candidates, but when Parker's and Pudeator's names were mentioned a second time, Warren collapsed into agonized fits.

Widow Parker's specter, she cried, had acknowledged bewitching Mary's sister and striking her dumb. The spirits of Parker and Pudeator seemed intent on outdoing each other to name all the people they had murdered, many of them at sea. Parker's, for example, boasted of wrecking Captain Thomas Westgate's ship.

The widow vehemently denied it. Trembling and crying, her young accuser then revealed a salient detail. Back before her sister had stopped speaking, Mary's father had promised to mow some of Alice Parker's meadow. Yet he failed to get to it, so the widow had come to their house and told him he had better do it or she would lose her crop. Thereafter, Mary claimed, first her sister and then her mother had taken ill; her parents soon died. Mary Warren's implication was not lost on the justices: that Alice Parker, whom neighbors had long suspected of witchcraft, had used diabolical powers to punish the family.

For effect, Mary added the usual claims: that Alice Parker's specter had confessed to joining other witches at a "Bloody Sacrament" in Reverend Parris's pasture. As it was, the orphaned maidservant couldn't come near Parker without collapsing into fits.

Another young accuser, Margaret Jacobs, supported Mary's claims. Even Marshal George Herrick, who had arrested Parker, confirmed in her presence that she had admitted seeing threescore witches at the dark assembly.

A few neighbors also had their say. John Westgate recounted the time that Alice had stormed into Samuel Beadle's tavern to hector her husband, John Parker, for drinking. When Westgate tried to placate her, she snapped at him and told him to keep his nose out of her business. So when the specter of a huge pig followed him and his dog across Salem that night as they walked home, he knew who had sent it.

Parker was also suspected of bewitching Samuel Shattuck's little boy, whose limbs and vitals were so bent and twisted that the physicians assumed it was witchcraft. A neighbor had tried some countermagic, and suddenly Parker was at the door paying a visit. When news of the Shattucks' suspicions got out, Alice and her husband marched over to the Shattuck home with a few men. Shattuck quickly changed his tune, insisting that he had never blamed Alice. But she wouldn't have it. "You are a wicked man!" Parker cried. "The Lord avenge me of you, the Lord bring vengeance upon you for this wrong!" When one of the men asked her why she had paid a visit to the Shattucks in the first place, she grew flustered. She had come to sell chickens, she finally said. But Shattuck pointed out that she had brought none with her. She had sold them to the neighbor, she quickly replied. But the neighbor, who happened to be among them, denied buying any. With all eyes upon her, Parker struggled to summon an explanation. Her son took the fowls to sea, she said. But her son had set sail the day *before* her visit, her husband pointed out. At that, Parker stormed into the adjoining room where Goodwife Shattuck sat with her sick son and scolded her for gossiping. "You are an evil woman," Parker exclaimed. "I hope I shall see the downfall of you!"

Perhaps the most damning testimony of all was the remark by Parker's own minister, Reverend Nicholas Noyes. He had visited her when she was ailing, he testified, and asked her whether she wasn't guilty of some of the malefic mischief attributed to her. Some evidence suggests that Alice may have been a stepdaughter of Giles Corey, a suspected wizard whose kinship to her would have been damaging enough. For whatever reason, nothing Parker could have said in her own defense would have made any difference, as the justices' minds were made up.

Since the Salem jail was filled to overflowing, she was sent to Boston. A jury of women stripped her, looking for suspicious nipples, but found none. Alice Parker was condemned nevertheless; on September 22, she hanged.

MARY PARKER, ANDOVER, 55

When she learned she had been accused of witchcraft, Mary assumed it a case of mistaken identity. It was a common name. Her husband's late brother, Joseph, had also wed a Mary, now elderly and increasingly senile.

But there was no mistake. Her own relative, Martha Sprague, made that clear when she announced, "This is the very woman."[7] Perhaps Goody Parker knew that it was only a matter of time. They had already arrested her twenty-two-year-old daughter, Sarah, two weeks before. Under questioning, Rebecca Eames had told the magistrates some gossip about Sarah's having been "kissed by the Devil" when crossed by love.

What would motivate such a cruel accusation was the biggest mystery, as Mary Ayer Parker was an upstanding member of Andover society. She was one of the founding generation, having moved to the Massachusetts Bay Colony from England, marrying the widower Nathan Parker at fifteen. They were pious, propertied folk who had worked hard. Her husband, a scribe, had drawn up most of the village's legal documents, while his brother, Joseph, ran a corn mill and tannery. When Nathan died in 1685, he left over 225 acres to her and their eldest son, John. He had done well by her.

They had tried to do well by their children. But they had also had their tragedies. One of their sons had been killed in 1677 while battling Indians in King Philip's War. A daughter, Hannah, had married John Tyler, whose family was plagued with misfortune. It had not escaped her notice that ever since the witchcraft trouble had spread to Andover in July, virtually every female in the Tyler family had been accused except for two: the wife and daughter of John's manipulative brother, Moses.

The authorities came for Mary on September 1. She was questioned the following day in a great spectacle watched by a throng of curious onlookers. A troupe of local girls, including members of her own extended family, Martha Sprague and Rose Foster, fell into a frenzy, requiring her touch to rid them of their violent fits. Some were from Salem. Mary Warren collapsed into such fits that blood ran out of her mouth. Asked if she hadn't cast a spell on three youths, Mary bristled. "I know nothing of it," she replied. "There is another woman of the same name in Andover."

At a touch test on September 7, her sister's daughter and granddaughter were arrested with other relatives; even more would be ensnared the following month. The court's ruling, when it came, was swift: Mary Parker was found guilty on September 17 and hanged five days later. But her sons persevered.

In November they posted a recognizance bond for the release of their cousin, Sarah Aslet, then issued a bluntly worded petition to the Salem court. In a stunning blow to Essex County sheriff George Corwin, the two described the sheriff's attempt to seize the family property. Cattle, corn, and hay had been taken from the farm, and the two were ordered to Salem to discuss the acreage with Corwin in person. After a lengthy debate, the sheriff offered them a truce: They could keep the land if they paid him a bribe. They bargained him from ten pounds down to six and kept the Parker farm. Their sister Sarah was eventually released.

JOHN PROCTOR, SALEM VILLAGE, 60

A shrewd businessman and tireless worker, he had earned himself an impressive estate. He knew enough not to get involved in the quagmire of Salem Village and kept his distance. Yet in the spring of 1692, a casual remark uttered there would destroy his life.

Riding into Salem Village, he had passed Samuel Sibley and stopped to chat. They got to talking about the witchcraft commotion, and Proctor mentioned that he was going in to pick up his maidservant, Mary Warren. She had been obsessed with demonic sightings, and against his better judgment, he had consented to bring her in the previous day to bear witness against Rebecca Nurse.

Now he regretted that decision and could not disguise his disgust at the girls' hysterics. If it were up to them, he remarked, "we should all be devils and witches quickly." What they really needed was a good whipping, he told Sibley, and Warren had one coming. When she had first acted up, he had kept her close to the spinning wheel. Her fits had eased until the following day, when he was called away and couldn't watch her. "Hang them!" Proctor muttered in exasperation. "Hang them!"

He would rue his words. Sibley, whose wife was among the many who believed that a cake containing a possessed person's urine could undo a witch's spell, told others of their chat. Eventually Sibley would stand up as a trial witness and relate their conversation. Proctor's wife was arrested in April, and a week later, he was as well.

Born in England, he had crossed the Atlantic with his parents and settled in Ipswich, Massachusetts. In 1666, while in his thirties, he fell upon an opportunity. A seven-hundred-acre farm southeast of the Salem Village line was up for grabs. The estate, known as Groton, had been built up over three decades by the esteemed Emmanuel Downing, whose brother-in-law, John Winthrop, was the Massachusetts Bay Colony's founder and first governor.

Proctor grabbed it, then in 1668 obtained a tavern license, which in those days were reserved for the upper crust. Proctor, by contrast, was neither a magistrate nor mill owner, though he was not without means. His father had bequeathed him a third of his substantial Ipswich property. By all accounts, John Proctor was a savvy entrepreneur, as comfortable selling to Indians as to Salem barons. It was in Salem that he went to church.

He managed the farm and property with his eldest son, Benjamin. Elizabeth, his third wife, had her hands full running the tavern and tending their eleven children, including six from his two previous marriages. No pushover, she demanded that customers short of cash pay in pawned goods. The Proctors' firmness served them well, even if it didn't endear them to their neighbors.

Since he was the first man accused of witchcraft that year, Proctor's hearing drew official attention. For the first time, a witchcraft interrogation was held in Salem instead of Salem Village. Conducting the proceedings would be Deputy Governor Thomas

Danforth, who rode up from Boston with a phalanx of dignitaries. But even the normally cautious Danforth let his sympathies for the anguished girls override his common sense.

A throng turned out to watch the show, and suspenseful it was. Abigail Williams and Ann Putnam Jr., looking terrified, pointed to Proctor's specter and crumpled to the floor in bloodcurdling screams. Some shouted that Proctor was flying to Bathshua Pope's feet, and sure enough, the woman's feet rose and she lurched backward.

Proctor defended himself, but the theatrics were so compelling that Danforth turned on him. "I would advise you to repentance," he scolded, "for the devil is bringing you out." Abigail Williams warned that others in the room would be hurt, and as if on cue, they started to writhe. When it was over, Danforth and his councilors caucused. After reviewing Reverend Samuel Parris's notes, they ordered that Proctor be taken into custody.

The next day, he and his wife were packed off to the Boston jail, and Salem's twenty-six-year-old sheriff, George Corwin, got busy. According to Boston merchant Robert Calef, Corwin drove a cart to Proctor's farm. He drained a beer barrel of its contents and rolled it away, emptied a pot of its broth and stashed it, and seized all the goods and foodstuffs he could find. He would sell some of the cattle at half their value; others he would slaughter, salt, and pack for shipment to the West Indies. In theory, an accused witch's belongings were to be used for his and his family's support until the time of his indictment, after which they could be confiscated by the Crown. Corwin was overly hasty, dividing the spoils on the assumption that the Proctors were doomed.

In late May, several members of Proctor's family were also detained, including Elizabeth's mother, Sarah Bassett, her sister, Mary Bassett DeRich, and her two oldest boys, Benjamin and William. The youngest children, including a three-year-old, were left in the care of their twenty-four-year-old half-brother, John, in a home stripped bare of provisions.

On May 31, the Proctors and seven others were transported from Boston to Salem prison for trial. Elizabeth had discovered she was pregnant, but on August 2, despite petitions signed in their defense, a jury found them guilty. At least Elizabeth's life would be spared until the child was born. John's would not.

In a last-ditch effort to save himself, John joined with other prisoners in penning a protest letter addressed to five Boston pastors. It complained that Proctor's son William and two others had been tortured to induce them to confess, and that the judges, jury, and accusers had condemned them before their trials. Proctor pleaded that the ministers support them in their efforts to persuade Governor Phips to either try them in Boston or replace the judges. Finally, it implored them to attend the upcoming trials, so that no more innocent blood would be shed.

He probably assumed such a desperate appeal would elicit some response. That it did not made him no more prepared to die for a crime he did not commit.

On the fateful day, August 19, John Proctor pleaded for a little more time, saying "he was not fit to die." None was granted, yet his courage and dignity were evident to all. One witness watching that day, Boston merchant Thomas Brattle, would write later that John Proctor and John Willard had shown astonishing strength: They had forgiven their accusers, demonstrated no malice toward the judges or juries, sought God's forgiveness for their sins, and shown themselves to be "very sincere, upright, and sensible of their circumstances on all accounts."

Elizabeth would survive him, as would her infant son, John. She would later discover that her husband's will had been changed before his death. She had been disinherited. In a 1696 petition to the court, she explained that "in that sad time of darkness before my said husband was executed it is evident som body had Contrived a will and brought it to him to sign."

The court must have agreed, as it granted her significant compensation.

ANN PUDEATOR, SALEM, 70

Perhaps they resented how easily she came into
wealth or suspected her of hastening her good fortune
by arranging her two husbands' deaths. A greater like-
lihood is that Ann Pudeator simply fell afoul of vicious
gossip. But if widowhood enriched her, it also left her
without a husband to shield her from the frenzied
slander the afflicted girls dreamed up.

Her demise began with a single angry remark. A
young neighbor, John Best, testified that the widow's
heated outburst had made him wonder if she might be
a witch. When rounding up his father's cattle, he had
often found her cow among them. Rather than bring
it home with the others, he would shoo it away. Pudeator would then "chide me when I Came houm," he
explained, "for turning the Cow bak."

In the 1650s and 1660s, she had settled in Falmouth,
Maine, with her first husband, Thomas Greenslade (or
Greenslit), with whom she had raised five children.
Before King Philip's War in 1675, they moved to Salem,
though two of her adult children stayed behind. After
her husband's death she had met Jacob Pudeator, a
blacksmith some twenty years her junior. After tending his ailing wife until her death in 1676, the two married, though he would follow her to the grave in 1682.

At her interrogation, Mary Warren suggested that
Ann had murdered her second husband's first wife,
then killed him as well by "giving him something
whereby he fell sick and dyed." Ann was also accused
of doing away with a neighbor's wife, causing a man

to fall out of a tree, turning into a bird and then flying into her house, and stabbing people with pins. Warren claimed that the widow kept ointments that she used to cast spells. Pudeator insisted it was simply grease for use in making soap.

Perhaps trying to help, Pudeator's Maine-based son, Thomas Greenslade Jr., stepped forward with evidence bolstering the case against Reverend George Burroughs. He had known the minister when both had lived in the Casco area and might have thought that cooperating with the judges could win his mother a reprieve. But his efforts came too late. Impatient to move ahead with the executions, on September 22, the court sent Ann Pudeator to her death.

Eighteen years later, the colony's General Court reversed the convictions, but Ann Pudeator's name was omitted from the list. It would take until 1957— almost two and a half centuries—before the Massachusetts State Legislature exonerated her.

WILMOT REED, MARBLEHEAD, 50s

"Mammy," as they called her, was the wife of Samuel Reed (also spelled Redd and Read), a poor fisherman. She was a familiar sight in the seaside village, doing odd jobs to make ends meet. Nothing is known of her children, if she had any, though a young woman, Martha Laurence, shared her home. Few other clues about Wilmot Reed have survived the centuries, apart from local lore.

Mammy, they said, had supernatural powers, which she readily channeled against her enemies. On a few occasions, she had willed that a "bloody cleaver" be found in certain infants' cradles; as soon as the curse was uttered, a vision of the bloodstained knife allegedly appeared. Soon after, a child would sicken and die. Her wickedness was legendary: She could make milk curdle in the pail and transform churned butter into blue wool.

None of her mischief had ever menaced anyone enough to summon the constable. Yet in May of 1692, a warrant arrived for Mammy Reed's arrest. In it she was charged with committing "sundry acts of witch craft" on two Salem girls she had never even met, Mary Walcott and Mercy Lewis. Her hands were bound and she was muscled into the back of an oxcart for the ten-mile trip to Salem Village.

At her interrogation, the possessed girls collapsed into hysterics. Several fell unconscious when she looked at them, though when Mammy grasped their arms, they sprang back to life. Urged to explain what she thought was ailing the girls, Mammy kept her temper in check, saying only, "I can not tell." When the magistrates insisted, she calmly replied, "My opinion is that they are in a sad condition."

She would wait four months in the stench and heat of Salem jail before the trial resumed that September. Marblehead constable James Smith appeared as a witness, claiming he had warned the other villagers about her. Salem's afflicted girls expressed their view that her behavior the previous May had effectively proven her guilt. But the magistrates wanted to hear from Marblehead witnesses. Fourteen had been summoned, though only three of their statements have survived.

They told the same tale. About five years before, a Mrs. Syms had been visiting from Salem. She had hired Mammy's "maid," Martha Laurence, to do domestic chores, and some linen had gone missing. She confronted Mammy about it, threatening to go to Salem and have Judge Hathorne issue a warrant for the girl's arrest unless they produced the goods.[8]

Infuriated, Mammy told her off. If she did not leave this instant, she hoped Mrs. Syms might never "mingere [urinate] nor cacare [defecate]." Sure enough, the affronted woman came down with a vile case of constipation that did not pass until she had left town. Deep down, Wilmot Reed must have savored the woman's distress, especially since Mrs. Syms, judging by her title, was probably a lady of means. Even so, the indignity of Mammy's taunts would come back to haunt her.

Mrs. Syms herself never appeared at the trial to substantiate the story, but it didn't matter. Hearsay was evidence enough. Mammy Reed denied the charges but was at the mercy of the court. No one stepped up to defend her, not Martha Laurence, not her Marblehead neighbors, not even her own husband. She was sentenced to hang, and on September 22, she did.

MARGARET SCOTT, ROWLEY, 77

Like Wilmot Reed, Margaret Scott was an easy target. An impoverished widow, only three of her seven
children had survived into adulthood. She lived on
donated land. Her husband, Benjamin, had been dead
for twenty-one years, and had left her a paltry inheritance. In desperation, she had stooped to asking neighbors for food and firewood, yet her pleas were largely
ignored.[9]

One well-heeled neighbor, the prominent Captain
Daniel Wycomb, had remarried after the death of his
first wife. His seventeen-year-old daughter, Frances,
was having difficulty adjusting to her new stepmother.
In April of 1692, not long after the first witch hearings were held in Salem, Frances was gripped with the
sensation of being choked. Her condition lasted into
the summer, and Widow Scott soon became the prime
suspect.

In late July, another Rowley girl, Mary Daniel,
felt a prickling in her feet as she sat by the fire, then
looked up to see Widow Scott floating toward her in
spectral form. The ghostly vision threw Mary from her
chair and onto the floor, leaving her speechless with
terror. Her encounters lasted nearly a week.

Then in August, twenty-two-year-old Sarah Coleman came under spectral attack. Widow Scott was
apprehended, interrogated, and jailed. At her September 15 trial, a group of Rowley witnesses attested to her
maleficence. Five years previously, they insisted, she
had orchestrated Robert Shilleto's long-term suffering

and subsequent death. She had put a curse on Captain Wycomb's oxen when he rebuffed her plea for corn, and sickened Thomas Nelson's cows when he refused to drop what he was doing to fetch her some firewood.

Her culpability was a foregone conclusion, a case promptly solved within Rowley's borders.

Unfortunately for Margaret Scott, her fate was clinched at an unfortunate juncture. Public criticism of the proceedings was growing; the justices were under pressure to rush the cases through before the trials were halted altogether. Most of the court documents are now missing, but it's almost certain that she refused to confess. Margaret Scott was found guilty. On September 22, she and seven other condemned prisoners were driven from Salem jail to Gallows Hill, where they were hanged.

ROGER TOOTHAKER, BILLERICA, 58

His diagnoses were largely guesswork. Before medical schools and anatomy books, the human body was uncharted territory. Ailments often couldn't be traced to anything rational and had to be explained away by the supernatural. Lacking any formal training beyond an apprenticeship to Dr. Samuel Eldred, Roger Toothaker would have used mystical folk remedies, as his peers did, and consulted the "Man of Signs" almanac for astrological guidance on balancing the bodily humors. He was the only physician accused of witchcraft in colonial New England.

While still a baby, he had sailed from London with his parents in 1635 and settled in Billerica, Massachusetts. His father died when he was four; the same year, his mother married Ralph Hill, and they moved to the Hill farm in the village's southern end.

At thirty-one, Roger married Mary Allen, the oldest child of a moderately prosperous Andover family. His stepfather had died a few years previously. The couple built a farm on land that might have been Roger's small inheritance. Though they had neighbors on all sides, to the north stretched four miles of open fields separating their English community from an Indian camp straddling the Merrimack River.

Mary had become a midwife, so for a time, they might have practiced together: he bandaging severed fingers, salving snake bites, and remedying worms, she delivering babies. Mary's younger sister, Martha, stayed home to watch the children until she married in 1674 and settled nearby.

For the next two years, King Philip's War raged around them, a harrowing time to be subsisting on the frontier with eight children. One of their sons, Allen, became a soldier and returned wounded. Then in 1683, the year their youngest, Margaret, was born, three family members died: their oldest son, Nathaniel, Roger's mother, and the second of two infants they had named Mary.

There were other practicing midwives by then, which might explain why Roger left his family for a time and moved to Salem. Perhaps he found it a lucrative place to set up a practice, at least until a direct competitor—Dr. William Griggs—arrived from Boston in 1690. Dr. Griggs's wife, Rachel Hubbard Griggs, was from an influential family. One of her kin, Elizabeth Hubbard, was living with them in 1692 when the witch hunt erupted. On May 18, Hubbard and two of her friends, Ann Putnam Jr. and Mary Walcott, named Roger Toothaker as a witch. He was arrested and sent to Boston jail the same day.

Within two weeks, all of Toothaker's female relatives had followed him to jail: his wife, Mary; his eldest daughter, Martha; his eight-year-old child, Margaret; and Mary's youngest sister, Martha Allen Carrier. The afflicted girls staged their usual melodrama, but during the interrogations, one piece of testimony resonated. Thomas Gage and Elias Pickworth recalled that a year before, they had gotten to talking with Dr. Toothaker about two sick boys. "He had seen them both already," they said, and concluded that "they were under an Evil hand." More damaging, however, was the doctor's comment that he had taught his eldest daughter, Martha Toothaker Emerson, how to kill a witch. The two men remembered every detail: "his Daughter gott some of the afflicted persons Urine and put it into an Earthen pott and stopt the pott very Close & putt said pott to a hott oven & stopt up said overn & the next morning said [witch, Mattheus Button] was Dead."

Roger Toothaker didn't survive his internment. On June 16, a coroner, Edward Wyllys, summoned twenty-four men to examine Toothaker's corpse. One of them, Benjamin Walker, reported that they had questioned those present at the time of his demise and concluded that "he came to his end by a natural Death."

He had spent his adulthood ministering to others, but when his own life was endangered, he was on his own.

SAMUEL WARDWELL, ANDOVER, 49

"I wonder how Wardwell could tell so true."

It was the thought on everyone's lips. Until John Bridges articulated it in 1692, Samuel Wardwell's fortune-telling had left the whole of Andover utterly mystified. The man was an oracle, capable of uncanny predictions that amused, amazed, and more unsettlingly, revealed a person's deepest secrets.

At Samuel Martin's house the previous winter, Wardwell had embarrassed young James Bridges by revealing his infatuation with a fourteen-year-old girl, something Bridges had never told a soul. Moreover, Wardwell had predicted that John Farnum would be spurned in love, that he would journey south, fall from his horse, and suffer a gunshot wound, all of which occurred. Wardwell boasted that he could will cattle to come to him, and he had been right about Ephraim Foster's wife: She would bear him five daughters before giving birth to a son. He would study a person's hand, look vacantly at the ground for a few moments, then expound on the person's future.

It had all been harmless fun until Joseph Ballard's wife fell ill in the spring of 1692. Nothing the doctor did could cure her. When her husband heard about the Salem Village afflictions, he started to wonder if Wardwell might be dabbling in the black arts and confronted him. Wardwell denied it, but several townsfolk suspected that only a sorcerer could predict the future with as much accuracy.

Then in August, Sarah Wardwell's fifty-year-old first cousin, Edward Marshall, died in Malden. Five days later, her thirty-four-year-old brother passed away in Reading, probably from a fever. The family laid his body out and procured the requisite gallons of wine for the next day's funeral, as it was hot and the body couldn't be kept. The Wardwells rode up from Andover, and late that night, the wine disappeared. Shouting could be heard, and suddenly the roof was ablaze. In the darkness, the voices took on a sinister tone, as if it had been the devil himself.

On August 15, Martha Sprague and her friends were at the Tylers' when they came under spectral assault. The apparitions, among them the Wardwells, forced the girls to dance and sing to the point of exhaustion. They coerced Rose Foster's mother into dancing about the house until she thought she would die.

Her husband, Andover constable Ephraim Foster, arrested Wardwell the same evening, leaving his wife, Sarah, alone with their seven children. But Martha Sprague and Rose Foster continued to suffer under Goody Wardwell's specter, so the constable returned a few weeks later to detain her as well. As a precaution, he also seized her two oldest daughters: nineteen-year-old Mercy Wardwell and twenty-one-year-old Sarah Hawkes, Sarah Wardwell's daughter from her previous marriage to the aged but affluent Adam Hawkes.

Secretly, the Fosters may have delighted in seeing Samuel Wardwell brought down. Until he married Sarah in 1673, he had been a penniless carpenter from Exeter, New Hampshire.[10] He had come up in the world, with extensive land holdings in Lynn, Massachusetts. He was also blessed with a large family, only one of their children dying in infancy. Since Rebecca, their youngest, was less than a year old and still nursing, she had gone with her mother to prison. But Wardwell had a problematic background. His father, Thomas, had been banished for heresy, and his brother Eliakim was a Quaker, living with his wife, Lydia, in New Jersey exile.

The Wardwells were questioned in Salem, and though Samuel hesitated at first, all four ultimately confessed. He had yielded to the devil, he said, out of discontent at the amount of work he managed to do, and because he had "foolishly" gotten into the habit of fortune-telling. Indeed, Andover witness Thomas Chandler testified that "he was much addicted to that and made sport of it."

Before it was over, Wardwell would admit to dark visions and lofty promises and a sinister man calling himself the Prince of Air. But the witchcraft trials had entered a new phase. So many had eagerly confessed— hoping it would save their lives—that the magistrates were growing suspicious. A month later, Wardwell would renounce the confession, as would his daughter, Mercy, but by then it was too late. Even he knew it, telling the grand jury that he realized he would die, whether he confessed or not. Lined up against him were not only the Salem and Andover afflicted, but more ominously, Andover selectmen Joseph Ballard and Thomas Chandler, and the town clerk and constable, Ephraim Foster. Suddenly the tables had turned, and it was the magistrates who were predicting the future: that on September 22, Samuel Wardwell would hang.

As the cart rattled him and seven others up to Gallows Hill that day, a wheel got stuck in the mud. As the guards got behind and pushed, some of the afflicted girls yelled that they could see the devil obstructing the cart's way. Eventually they freed it and continued on.

One by one, the condemned were forced up the ladder, their hands and feet bound, and told to utter their last words. Samuel Wardwell was declaring his innocence when the executioner's pipe smoke drifted into his face and made him cough. Again the afflicted girls shouted taunts, saying the devil was attempting to silence him.

Five days later, Andover's selectmen sought authorization to place the Wardwells' four "suffering" children, who had been abandoned, in separate foster homes. The two oldest girls were tried, acquitted, and released. Their mother's death sentence was commuted. After five months in jail, the women returned home to find it looted.

To cover trial expenses, the sheriff and his deputies had seized everything they could move, including five cows, a heifer and a yearling, a horse, nine hogs, eight loads of hay, and Samuel's carpentry tools, along with six acres of corn. In a final gesture, the authorities refused to reverse Sarah's attainder, the post-conviction order that had stripped her of all civil rights, including land ownership and bequests. Her property in Lynn, the last of her remaining assets, was confiscated.

SARAH WILDES, TOPSFIELD, 65

Not everyone rejoiced when John Wildes, a prosperous Topsfield farmer, announced his engagement to Sarah Averill. For one thing, it had hardly been a year since his wife, Priscilla Gould Wildes, had passed away. Her sister, Mary Gould Reddington, couldn't comprehend what John saw in Sarah, a brash and ostentatious creature who paraded around in clothing far above her station. Besides, it was hardly a secret that some years before, Sarah had received a public whipping for fornication.

It was true that Sarah could be abrasive. She quarreled with her neighbors, some of whom suspected that she employed witchcraft to avenge perceived wrongs.

The two were married, after which Mary confided to her neighbors of her new sister-in-law's personal flaws. Sarah was furious, and the two had a heated confrontation. By 1663, John Wildes had grown so tired of Mary's constant criticism that he took her husband aside and threatened to sue unless it ceased.

At Sarah's trial some thirty years later, Reverend John Hale of Beverly described the ensuing discussion. Mary's husband, distressed at the thought of a family lawsuit, cautioned Wildes against it. Legal fees would only waste his estate, he reasoned, and besides, his wife "would [be] done with it in tyme." John Wildes never did sue, but stories of Sarah's malefic adventures continued unabated. Among other things, she was blamed for killing livestock and bewitching cartloads of hay to even the score against their owners.

When the Salem witch trials convened in 1692, the old stories sprang to mind. Though Mary Reddington

was long dead, her grievances lived on. At Sarah's interrogation, Reverend Samuel Parris wrote in his notes
that "she was charged by some [with] hurting John
Herricks [step]mo[ther]," Mary Gould Reddington.[11]

Reverend Hale described Mary's visit, and how
she had "opened her griefs to him" and confided that
Sarah was bewitching her. He wondered if Sarah might
also be afflicting her own stepson Jonathan, one of
eight children from Wildes's first marriage. The boy
had behaved so oddly that Hale convened several area
pastors to pray for him. Some thought the boy might
be mentally ill or diabolically possessed, but most suspected he was playacting. They would never know, as
Jonathan died in the Indian wars.

Other gossip surfaced, most of it secondhand. A
neighbor, Elizabeth Symonds, spoke at length about
Sarah's threats after her two brothers had "borrowed"
her scythe without Sarah's permission. The scything
done, they attempted to move a cartload of hay they
had mowed with it, but the oxen wouldn't budge. Then
a wheel fell off the cart, and they had to dump all the
hay to fix it. More mishaps ensued. Spooked by an
odd-looking dog, the oxen stampeded into the brook,
sending the entire load tumbling into the water.

It didn't help that Sarah had already been tried for
witchcraft in 1676, though she was acquitted of the crime,
or that the Salem accusers suffered fits at the mere sight
of her. One of them, Deliverance Hobbs, swore she had
seen Sarah's spirit among "a great many birds, cats, &
dogs," and that Sarah "tore me almost to pieces."

The magistrates found the show convincing enough
to convict her, and on July 19, Sarah Wildes hanged.

John Willard, Salem Village, 20s

In the spring of 1692, it was John Willard's turn to be constable.

Among his responsibilities was riding out to the homes of accused witches, shackling them, and bringing them to jail. But their numbers grew so drastically that at some point he couldn't bring himself to arrest any more, so he handed in his staff. Soon after, he learned that Ann Putnam Jr. had accused him of witchcraft.

At first he seemed mystified that she would do such a thing. Indeed, his wife's grandfather, Bray Wilkins, described how "greatly troubled" he looked when he stopped by to ask if they would pray for him. Wilkins, citing a previous engagement, was unable to oblige.

Then on May 4, Wilkins saw him at a Boston dinner party. Willard, who arrived in the company of one of Wilkins's sons, gazed peculiarly at the patriarch, in a way that no one ever had before. Stepping into an adjacent room, Wilkins suddenly felt stricken, unable to eat or urinate, feeling, as he would later describe it, "like a man in a Rack." Immediately he sensed that "Willard had done me wrong."

A woman healer later examined him, asking whether "those evil persons" involved in the witchcraft flare-up hadn't "done him damage."

Though still experiencing pain a few days later, Wilkins managed the thirty-mile trip home, only to find that one of his grandsons, seventeen-year-old Daniel, had fallen seriously ill with an unexplained disease. Not long before, Daniel had impetuously remarked that "it were wel If the sayd Willard were hanged." In a week, the boy was dead, a tragedy for which Wilkins could find only one explanation: Willard had bewitched him. Wilkins's urine soon turned bloody, he testified later, and "the old pain returned excessively."

Mindful that he would soon be arrested, Willard made for the hills, but a search party quickly set out after him. Their determination to bring him to justice suggests that Willard was deemed responsible for crimes far more serious than refusing to arrest witch suspects.

Much of his background remains obscure. Willard spent part of his youth in Lancaster, which suggests he might have been one of the seventeen children born to Major Simon Willard, a prominent fur trader and politician who owned property there. After marrying one of Wilkins's granddaughters, Margaret Knight, the couple moved to Groton, where Simon Willard had lived until his 1676 death. From there they moved to Salem Village.

Initially Willard worked as a hired hand and jack-of-all-trades on Thomas Putnam's farm. Ann Putnam Sr. had just given birth to a daughter, and the newcomer was occasionally tasked with watching her and the other children. But the infant died before her first birthday. Her grieving parents and their daughter, Ann, blamed Willard for her death.

The conflict didn't keep the Putnams from their friendship with the rest of the Wilkins clan.[12] The two families banded together in the drive to break away from Salem and establish their own church in Salem Village. Later, they would stand united in defending their disgraced pastor, Samuel Parris.

The Wilkinses lived in a cluster of houses at "Will's Hill" on Salem Village's western edge. By marrying John Willard, Margaret became the first in three generations to break with the family's tradition of wedding Salem Village farmers. Not only was Willard an outsider, but he saw little merit in subsistence farming. In 1690 he and three partners purchased a vast tract on Salem Village's northern border from George Corwin's widow, planning to divide it into parcels and sell them at a profit.

Bray Wilkins would have discouraged such speculation, as he had gotten burned in a similar venture years before. In 1658 Wilkins had invested in a timber-processing operation. He and a partner had taken out a mortgage on the seven hundred acres surrounding Will's Hill and begun churning out boards, barrel staves, and shingles, but profits proved elusive. To his great shame, he was caught stealing hay to feed his oxen. His house burned in 1664, and he had to return two-thirds of the land. His farm on Will's Hill was the one thing he managed to retain, so by the 1680s, he had returned to the safety of subsistence farming.

The old man must have bitterly resented Willard's business success. The Putnams would have sympathized with Wilkins, having lost their own shirts in a failed ironworks. So when a posse was formed to round up Willard, six of its ten horsemen were Putnams.

They caught up with him in Lancaster, hoeing one of his meadows. The moment he was brought in to the Salem Village watchhouse, Ann Putnam Jr. and other afflicted girls suffered such violent seizures that Willard had to be shackled.

At Willard's May 18 interrogation, Judge Hathorne reminded him that his escape attempt was a virtual admission of guilt. Willard replied that he had fled out of fear, but was innocent of witchcraft. Several neighbors testified against him. Ann Putnam Sr. charged him with murdering thirteen villagers. Asked if he had harmed Bray Wilkins, Willard rambled until the magistrate cut him off, saying, "We do not send for you to preach."

Of all the alleged slayings, Daniel Wilkins's death was the most mysterious. The village's new constable, John Putnam, had twelve men examine the body. Much of the boy's back seemed "pricked with an instrument about the bigness of a small awl." His throat was bruised all the way up to the ear, and when the body was turned over, blood spurted from the nose or mouth, yet there was no swelling or vomit that might signal poison. In their view, the boy had died "an unnatural death by some cruel hands of witchcraft or diabolical act."

Benjamin Wilkins, Bray's youngest son, maintained that Willard had beaten his wife so hard that he had broken the sticks he was using. Willard called him a liar and said his wife would confirm it, but the magistrate refused to summon her. They subjected him to a touch test, but failed to break him. It was only at the close of the interrogation, when he attempted to recite the Lord's Prayer, that his confidence wavered. Five times he tried, stumbling each time. He uttered a nervous laugh: "It is a strange thing, I can say it at another time. I think I am bewitcht as well as they." Judge Hathorne pressed him to confess, but he refused.

His wife brought him food during his imprisonment, even traveling as far as Boston when he was transferred to the jail there. She would later petition the court on his behalf. Though short of money, she hired a horse and rode it to Boston to inquire into the court's delay in rendering a decision, but her efforts proved futile.

On August 19, Willard and four other condemned witches were carted to Gallows Hill for execution.

If his nerve had failed him in court, it sustained him now.[13] In his diary, Samuel Sewall remarked at how convincingly Willard had spoken, how his words had moved hearts, and at how well he had died.

After Willard's death, Bray Wilkins's bladder problems subsided. He would outlive the much younger man by ten years, dying in 1702, still impoverished, at ninety-two.

CHAPTER 3

THE CLERGY

Religion was the glue that held Massachusetts together. As its steward, the minister was the community's leading citizen and primary source of inspiration and learning. It was he who ministered to the sick, prayed with the dying, presided at funerals (magistrates performed weddings), and resolved local and even regional disputes, often in concert with other clergymen. Working as the schoolmaster in villages that had at least fifty families, he taught the boys to read and cipher.

Though his duties did not extend into governance, his influence usually did, seeing as his chief purpose was to keep the community on its spiritual course. The colony was founded, after all, to be a religious sanctuary and utopia, a truly pure Christian society.

Starting at sundown on Saturday, villagers laid down their axes and hoes and returned home for evening prayers. Drinkers were shooed from taverns, farmers from the fields. Working or even traveling on a Sunday was a violation of the Sabbath, a punishable offense, unless the traveler was on his way to or from the meetinghouse.

Attendance was compulsory. Women were seated on one side, men on the other; a tithingman woke those who dozed off, and children were put together in a place where they could be watched, sometimes in the back or in the balcony, with the servants and slaves. The meetinghouse was usually a plain wooden structure, bereft of the slightest adornment. In winter it was a chilly, unheated place. The groaning wooden benches proved hard on people's backs. No whispering, smiling, or daydreaming was tolerated. The congregation bowed their heads, prayed, and sang hymns, but mostly they spent the day listening to sermons.

As grueling as it could be, most welcomed the Sabbath. It was a break from work, an opportunity to exercise the mind instead of the back, and a chance to chat—during the mid-day break, anyway—and take stock of the community.

Though he was greatly respected, the minister was at the mercy of his flock. He relied on his parishioners for firewood and compensation, received partly in coins, partly in "country pay," which could end up as corn, apples, honey, or pigs' feet. Most planted their own gardens and fields. Taxed to the breaking point during the Indian wars, some parishioners had no choice but to pay their annual contribution in labor, by haying or chopping wood. But salaries often went unpaid for months, even years, and there was always a struggle over the rights to the parsonage.

If he owned it, at least a clergyman would have a place to live when he got old and frail. If fired—which was rare, since most ministers served for life—he would be homeless until he found another position. Some solved the housing problem by marrying well-heeled widows and moving in with them. Others, like Samuel Parris, would spend years haggling and negotiating and still be consumed by financial worries.

But none doubted the existence of witches. For one thing, it was enshrined in the Bible; Exodus 22:18 cites it plain and simple: "Thou shalt not suffer a witch to live."

But their conviction went even deeper. In the Puritan view, the devil's kingdom was the heavenly realm reversed. The evil prince was always recruiting followers, just as God was. Any deluded, foolish, or unscrupulous woman could be lured into his trap by promises of silk or ribbons or carefree days. Ultimately it was an unfair trade-off. She would find herself being brutally exploited, a vehicle for the supernatural powers the devil conferred. Some ministers believed it more literally than others.

But belief in Satan, a fallen angel bent on destroying God's empire, was a corollary of Protestantism. It supplied the fear that might compel wayward souls to forsake sin and choose the path of goodness. Any misgivings about the existence of one spiritual extreme only cast doubt on the other. Since witches served the devil, not to believe in their existence was akin to heresy. Besides, what else was the clergy for if not to guide and protect people from the devil's clutches?

Thomas Barnard, Andover, 34

He was a conscientious preacher, fresh from divinity school and eager for a parish of his own. Yet for all his good intentions, Thomas Barnard seemed inexplicably plagued. For each of his triumphs, he was dealt a defeat. He must have anguished over God's message. Was his soul destined for salvation, as ministers' were assumed to be, or doomed to eternal damnation?

The cycle started in 1682, the year he was called to the Andover pulpit. He was twenty-four. He had graduated from Harvard in 1679 and had been teaching in Roxbury's ramshackle schoolhouse since 1680. He would be sharing the Andover pastorate with sixty-six-year-old Reverend Francis Dane, who had preached in the village for thirty-four years. Dane was too lame to meet his clerical obligations, yet he seemed reluctant to leave.

His ambivalence left Barnard in an awkward position. While the young preacher looked forward to assuming his new responsibilities, he was less enthralled about having a disapproving elder forever looking over his shoulder. Indeed, Dane had been so upset at the prospect of relinquishing his salary that he had filed a lawsuit against the church.

A council of ministers had been summoned to smooth things out. According to the agreement, Dane would receive thirty pounds a year, Barnard fifty. The parishioners would supply both ministers with a house and firewood. Upon Dane's death, Barnard would receive the entire amount, eighty pounds. It seemed reasonable enough, though some parishioners were rankled at having to pay two salaries.

With his spacious house and land, Dane was already comfortable, while the untested Barnard was not. The senior minister's bum legs kept him from going out to pray with the ill and dying and from performing other pastoral duties. Yet Dane's seniority was undiminished, a situation made all the more vexing due to the wide gap in their religious philosophies.

Barnard, the son of a maltster, was born in Hartford, Connecticut, and raised in the wilderness outpost of Hadley, Massachusetts. From the start, he had been schooled in orthodox Puritan dogma. As he saw it, most things in life could be neatly classified as either good or evil. Dane, on the other hand, dwelled in a shadowy world of moral in-betweens. He even questioned the existence of witches. In 1665 he had demonstrated as much when he testified that a devious herdsman, John Godfrey, was innocent of witchcraft.

Most had disagreed, yet Godfrey was freed. Twenty years had come and gone, and Thomas Barnard wished nothing more than to get on with his new position. Within two years, he would be celebrating a new triumph, his marriage to Elizabeth Price. She was the stepdaughter of magistrate Dudley Bradstreet, Andover's most prominent resident, Governor Simon Bradstreet's son. By 1692 they had two young sons and a new home in the north part of the village, just north of the Bradstreet mansion.

That spring, witchcraft broke out all over Salem, filling the province with panic. Understandably, Dane stayed mum: Four of his relatives were among the accused. But as Barnard saw it, a principle was at stake. Here was an opportunity for him to demonstrate his moral authority. So when one of his flock brought two of Salem Village's afflicted girls to Andover to search for witches, the junior minister observed. He called the villagers to a meeting on September 7 and, after offering an opening prayer, allowed the girls free rein to do their work. The ensuing witch-finding "touch-test" unmasked seventeen Andover women, among them Deliverance Dane, who was married to Reverend Dane's son, Nathaniel.

Soon all of Andover was in a panic. Local girls started screaming and falling into convulsive fits; villagers rode to town to accuse their neighbors. Some of the accused were probably questioned at Barnard's home, at a safe distance from Reverend Dane. With so many of his family members implicated, the senior minister could no longer act as an impartial observer. Though Dane himself had yet to be formally accused, virtually all of his female relatives were.

Yet if Barnard thought Dane's predicament would mean an end to pulpit sharing, he was wrong. Instead of capitulating, the old man mobilized. In October Barnard signed his name to one of Francis Dane's petitions. From that point onward, he supported Dane in a courageous effort to bring an end to the scapegoating and free the detained. If the two pastors had been estranged before, their battle to contain Andover's witch hunt might have bonded them. The crisis ended, and none of Dane's immediate family members were harmed.

But just when Barnard might have enjoyed a sense of triumph, tragedy struck him down. A year after the trials ended, his wife died unexpectedly, probably from childbirth, around the time that their third son, Theodore, was born. Four years later, Barnard remarried, this time to Abigail Bull, who would look after his three motherless sons. He served five more years yoked with Reverend Dane, fifteen in all under the older man's tutelage. A contemporary, Samuel Phillips, would later describe the junior parson as a "grave and instructive" man, prudent in his conduct, yet "meek and quiet," though cheerful in conversation.

He delivered excellent sermons, demanded discipline in the church, and wrote meticulous diary entries on his boys' education, as well as the contributions his parishioners made toward his salary. He noted the plowing and hay carting done for him by the humbler members of the congregation, for instance, along with the more substantial contributions by the well-heeled, such as the eight ewes he received from Simon Bradstreet.

After Dane's death in 1697, Barnard came into his own. He would narrowly escape an Indian attack on Andover in 1698, but if there was any gratification in having the pulpit to himself, it was tempered by grief. His second wife died in 1702, followed by his third, the widowed Lydia Goffe, two years later. Then in 1707, the parsonage burned to the ground. Having lost all three of his wives, he was now homeless as well, with three sons to care for. And owing to a political dispute, his salary hadn't been paid.

The brouhaha was over the meetinghouse. Andover was long overdue for a new one, but the congregation could not agree where to build it. The old one had stood at the center of a cluster of homes in Andover's northern half. But by 1707, at least sixty percent of the population was living in the south. Unable to mend the rift, the community appealed to the colony's government.

A year later, the General Court returned a ruling: The village would be divided into two parishes, north and south. Barnard was so disenchanted that he declared a day of lamentation. He would lose eighty south-end parishioners. The original north parish, where he resided, was the smaller of the two, and now they were asking him to name his pulpit. Would he serve in the north or in the south? It stupefied him. For eleven months, he stalled, lodged in a temporary home that the village had fortified for protection against Indian attacks. In frustration, the south parish petitioned the government to impose a deadline. If Reverend Barnard did not announce his preference by December of 1710, the south-enders would "provide for themselves."

The deadline passed, and Barnard still could not bring himself to choose. Soon the news was out that twenty-two-year-old Samuel Phillips was the south's new parson. He would serve the parish for sixty years.

As consolation, the village patched together a grant so that Barnard could own his own residence. By 1715 his new homestead was complete.[1] It was a handsome one in the saltbox style, with a gaping central fireplace and heavy timbered ceilings. Now fifty-seven, he moved in with his six beds, five tables, two chests, fourteen chairs, his books, spinning wheels, his gun, and his powder horn. His eleven head of cattle, his oxen and his sheep grazed out back.

He would enjoy his new house, but only for three years. Having weathered a witch hunt and lost half his parish, he was weary. To his credit, he had recruited 273 new members and merged the men's and women's sections, so that the two sexes sat together. In 1718, at the age of sixty, he died of apoplexy.[2] He would score one final triumph, but never live to savor it: John Barnard, his twenty-eight-year-old son, would succeed him as North Andover's minister.

Francis Dane, Andover, 76

His signature was squat and uneven, the *F* curling whimsically at both ends. At the time of the witch trials, Andover's senior minister had cut back his duties due to ill health. The nature of his sermons remains a mystery, as none have survived. Yet an intensely private poem he penned still exists, one he had probably tucked inside the pages of a book where he thought no one would discover it. The picture it paints is of a lonely man longing for a like-minded companion.

Like so many in seventeenth-century Massachusetts, he had lost his first two wives. As Andover's model citizen and holiest divine, Francis Dane was more like an affable neighbor than a scholar. Yet this arthritic, avuncular elder had such a powerful grip on his parishioners that instead of confronting him directly with their grievances, they took it out on his kin. Before the witch hunt was over, twenty-six members of his extended family would be accused, including two of his daughters and five of his grandchildren. Two of his nieces would hang. No other single family was hit so hard.

Born in Bishop's Stortford, England, he studied at King's College, Cambridge, before crossing the Atlantic in 1636 to join his parents and brother in Roxbury, Massachusetts. Six years after his mother's death there in 1642, the now thirty-three-year-old bachelor was ordained as Andover's second minister. He married Elizabeth Ingalls of Lynn, Massachusetts, and moved into a parsonage a few minutes' walk from the meeting-house. The colony's future governor, Simon Bradstreet, would become a close friend and neighbor.

Both were cautious, thoughtful men, reluctant to make hasty judgments. They would both be called to court in 1665, when an Andover squatter and ne'er-do-well, Job Tyler, accused his hired hand, John Godfrey, of witchcraft. In Dane's court testimony, he acknowledged that Godfrey was an "ill-disposed" person but rejected any notion that he could be involved with the supernatural. Judge Simon Bradstreet agreed and acquitted the man.

Over the years, Godfrey and Tyler continued their legal battle, but life in Andover was good. The Danes had four girls and two boys. Then in 1676, during the worst of the first Indian war, Elizabeth died. He would marry twice more, outliving his second wife, Mary Thomas, who died in 1689, then exchanging vows with his stepsister, Hannah Abbot, the following year.[3]

When he reached sixty-five, Reverend Dane announced that due to bodily infirmities, he would teach school but cease to preach "on a regular basis." Thomas Barnard was hired as his replacement, after which Dane's salary was abruptly cancelled. The village hoped "he might subsist without becoming burdensome to them."

But that was out of the question. Dane had been vocal before when his salary had been neglected or underpaid, and he was now, sparking a dispute so intractable that the selectmen had to appeal to Boston

for help. The General Court sent a group of ministers and magistrates to mediate, and a solution was
reached: Dane would receive an annual salary of
thirty pounds, Barnard fifty pounds, and both would
be supplied with stores of firewood. In a final caution-
ary word, the court advised Dane to resume his tasks,
"forgetting all former disgusts," or the villagers might
begrudge him the money.

Perhaps they already did. With his children grown,
he and his wife had a comfortable house to themselves.
Their sizeable property had been donated by the town.
The parishioners furnished them with wheat and
corn, since grain was the currency with which most
of his salary was paid. He socialized with the upper
crust, and while his parishioners labored in the fields,
Dane led a relatively leisurely existence of teaching,
study, and prayer. Barnard, no doubt, was left with the
thankless jobs, such as praying with the bedridden and
clearing drunkards from the tavern before sundown
on Saturday, the start of the Sabbath.

When the witchcraft panic descended on Andover in July 1692, it was largely self-inflicted. Joseph
Ballard, fretting over his wife's lingering fever, had
ridden down to Salem Village to fetch two of the tormented girls. They looked in on his wife and confirmed his fears that she had been bewitched, then
went door to door to identify other suspects. In the
most egregious act of all, they staged a "touch test" at
the meetinghouse. The neighborhood women were
lured in, blindfolded, then made to touch the writhing
girls. If their convulsing ceased, it was proof that the

woman had compromised herself to the devil. By the time it was over, seventeen had been arrested, including Deliverance, the wife of Dane's son Nathaniel.

By September 17, forty-eight Andover women were in custody, more than any other town. Dane's own family was hit the worst: two of his daughters, the wife of one of his two sons, and several of his grandchildren, not to mention nieces, nephews, and extended kin. A few of the afflicted had even hinted that the senior minister himself was the cause of their pains, but no one dared accuse him by name. With the execution that August of Reverend George Burroughs, Dane would have been acutely aware that his life was in danger.

But that didn't stop him. In a long and tireless effort, he persuaded Barnard and twenty-three others to sign a series of petitions, appeals, and letters to government officials and influential pastors. He coached his imprisoned daughter Abigail Faulkner through the rhetorical minefield of interrogations and trials. Ingeniously, she submitted to their authority without ever admitting guilt. The court condemned her, but being pregnant, her execution was postponed. By the time her child was born, the crisis was over, and she was freed.

In a strongly worded letter to the General Court dated January 2, 1693, Dane rejected suggestions that Andover had been rife with sorcery. "Had charity been put on, the Devil would not have had such an advantage against us," he wrote, "and I believe many innocent persons have been accused and imprisoned.

Ye conceit of specter evidence as an infallible mark did too far prevail with us. Hence we so easily parted with our neighbors of an honest and good report and members in full communion; hence we so easily parted with our children when we knew nothing in their lives nor any of our neighbors [to suspect them], and thus things were hurried on."

Most of all, he came down on the court for failing to put a stop to the excesses. "Our sin of ignorance, wherein we thought we did well," he wrote, "will not excuse us when we know we did amiss."

If Dane's enemies hoped to use the witch hunt to bring down the obstinate clergyman, they woefully underestimated him. In its aftermath, his courage and tenacity probably won him even greater authority and respect. Francis Dane remained Andover's senior minister until his death in 1697, at the age of eighty-two.

JOHN HALE, BEVERLY, 56

As a boy of twelve, John Hale joined the throngs gaping at the pitiful spectacle of Margaret Jones, a convicted witch. Not long after, the woman was fitted with a noose and hanged, her limp body dangling from a Boston scaffold. It was a sight he never forgot.

For the rest of his life, witchcraft would both fascinate and repel him. As a minister consigned to saving souls, something drove him to study and observe the witchcraft cases. When a storm of sorcery swept through Salem Village in 1692, John Hale was drawn in both as a participant and observer. He was a constant presence at the trials, taking notes and recording testimony. Yet until his own wife was accused, it never dawned on Hale that the trials and executions might be fatally flawed.

He was born in Charlestown in 1636, the only son of a blacksmith who had migrated from England in 1630 and married a Boston woman. A deacon of the Charlestown church, Hale's father probably encouraged him to enter the ministry. He studied theology at Harvard, graduating in 1657, two years before his father's death. Ten years later, he would be ordained as the first minister in Beverly, where he would remain until his death in 1700.

Whenever a case of witchcraft cropped up, Hale showed up to observe. In 1679, twelve years after taking the pulpit, one of his own parishioners would be accused, the aged Elizabeth Morse of Newbury. Years later he would note that though the jury had found her guilty, Governor Simon Bradstreet had reprieved her, "being unsatisfied in the verdict."

Like Bradstreet, Hale never doubted the existence of witches. What concerned him was whether the court had adequately proven the suspect's guilt. But whereas Bradstreet preferred to err on the side of caution, Hale's priority was to root witches out. For him, even the casual use of the devil's name was a cause for alarm.

But idle threats were the least of Hale's private worries. His first two wives would predecease him, as would two of his six children. His first marriage, in 1664, was to Rebecca Byley. It would last nineteen years and produce two children, Rebecca and Robert. A year after her death in 1683, Hale married Sarah Noyes. Her father, Reverend James Noyes, assisted at Newbury's meetinghouse, and her cousin, Reverend Nicholas Noyes, at Salem's. Sarah Hale bore her husband a girl and three boys, the last of which was born in December of 1692, as the witch frenzy was tapering off. Her pregnancy had been worrisome, as rumors started flying about that she was a witch and that her specter had tormented unwitting people, including Mary Herrick of Wenham. Hale visited Herrick in November to hear her out.

He had spent the entire year listening. He had listened to the confessors, to the afflicted, to the judges, and to other clergymen. He had tried not to dismiss their assertions out of hand. But Mary Herrick's remarks jarred him. It was not that he suspected that his own wife could be a witch. Of her innocence, he didn't have the slightest doubt. What troubled him was the notion that the devil might have been masquerading himself under the identities of innocent people. If so, he realized, the witch court might have inadvertently executed twenty innocent people.

On Christmas Eve in 1692, Sarah Hale safely gave birth to a son. She named him John, after her husband. After her death five years later, Hale married for the third and last time. This wife, Elizabeth Somerby, would survive him. In 1698, the same year of their wedding, he finished a history of the Salem witch trials, *A Modest Enquiry into the Nature of Witchcraft*. It was published in 1702, two years after his death, with an introduction by Salem's sympathetic minister, Reverend John Higginson, whose own family had been plagued by unfounded accusations.

Though he never apologized for having backed the trials, Hale felt compelled to explain what prompted his change of heart. His belief in Satan never faltered, but he conceded that as the accusations piled up, he found it harder to believe that "so many in so small a compass of land should so abominably leap into the Devil's lap at once." Some of the accused were clearly faultless, he wrote, and the general population began to doubt the court. Ultimately, the afflicted accusers went too far.

Perhaps the reason that he chose to have his book published posthumously was concern that it would cause the family grief. After all, his beloved second wife's cousin, the seemingly amiable Reverend Nicholas Noyes, had staunchly defended the prosecutions.

While not wishing to offend, Hale felt a need to set the record straight. He too had defended the trials until the end, even acting as a witness. In September of 1692, he had been summoned to testify about one of his more rowdy parishioners, Dorcas Hoar, who was suspected of witchcraft.

The Court of Oyer and Terminer was trying her case. Hale was summoned to Salem to give evidence and had little good to say. Hoar had always enjoyed telling fortunes, usually predicting the deaths of family members. He had chastised her for it, but to no avail. Then in 1678, Hoar and her family had conspired with one of Hale's maidservants, Margaret Lord. Together they had robbed the Hale household of clothing, food, livestock, money, even a pudding bag. They had stolen a necklace one pearl at a time and swiped pillowcases of flour at every opportunity.

When the Hales were away, Margaret had invited Hoar's daughters to the parsonage and entertained them. To keep the Hales' children from telling, Margaret threatened to summon the devil or even kill the Hales. To press the point, Margaret had picked up a large book and shown it to his eldest child, thirteen-year-old Rebecca. The Hoars would raise the devil against her with this book, Margaret claimed. At other times, the servant had dangled Rebecca over the well and threatened to burn her with a hot pan.

When the Hales started to notice that things were missing, Margaret took flight. It was then that Rebecca mustered the courage to tell her father. After Hale notified the authorities and the couple was fined, the

Hoars began a malicious retaliatory siege against Beverly's minister. Dorcas's husband, William, openly threatened him. They felt thumping noises against the house at random hours, and in the worst assault of all, the Hoar children clubbed the Hales' cow to death.

Earlier that summer, Hale had visited Dorcas Hoar in prison to question her about her strange knack for predicting people's deaths. After her husband had died that winter, some had implied that Dorcas had killed him. What Hale didn't realize until a friend told him much later was the terror that his daughter Rebecca had suffered from the Hoars' mischief. By then it was too late to discuss it with her, as she had died two years after the episode, at the age of fifteen.

Dorcas Hoar maintained her innocence but was sentenced to death. When she finally confessed, Hale and three other pastors pleaded with the court to delay her execution. Judge Bartholomew Gedney granted their request, reprieving her the day before her scheduled hanging.

In later years, while the people of Salem Village were withholding Reverend Samuel Parris's pay, Beverly was rewarding Reverend Hale, their beloved spiritual guide, with a bonus for his years of faithful service.[4]

JOHN HIGGINSON, SALEM, 76

Had it not been for a storm, he would have lived the rest of his life back home in England. Forty bitter years of New England wilderness had been quite enough. But high winds swelled the waves just as the ship was setting out off the Massachusetts coast. For safety's sake, they pulled into Salem harbor, and John Higginson never left.

He had come to the colonies in 1629 with his parents and eight siblings. His Cambridge-educated father, Francis Higginson, had been the minister at Claybrooke, a town in the English Midlands. Disillusioned with the Anglican Church, his father had associated with dissident preachers, including Thomas Hooker. Then in 1628, the Massachusetts Bay Company invited him to join them in their quest to build a better society in America.

The family set sail in May of the following year. There would be three hundred of them in five vessels, including many from their home congregation. They rowed ashore to a Salem of six crude shacks; John's father became the tiny settlement's first minister. But the snows were harsh that winter, and many fell sick. Before spring, his father would die of fever at the age of forty-three. Being thirteen and the eldest boy, it was up to John to support the family.

At first they went to Boston, where he studied for the ministry and worked as a scribe. Eventually they would move on to Connecticut. For about four years, Higginson served as chaplain at the fledgling Saybrook

Colony that John Winthrop Jr. had established in what is now Old Saybrook. Later Higginson would move to Hartford, where he worked as a schoolmaster, and then to Guilford, where he would marry Sarah Whitfeld and succeed her father as parson.

He had every intention of returning to England when he set sail in 1659. Waylaid by the storm, Higginson renewed old acquaintances, who persuaded him to stay on for a year and preach. It must have struck him as providential that the very church his father had established was now turning to him in supplication, as if to fulfill his father's mission. So he consented, leaving his brother to sail on to England without him.

He was ordained a year later and would preach there until his death in 1708. The intervening years were mostly good. He had been hard on the Quakers, a stance he would later regret. So when the farmers to the east split off to form their own church, only to be inundated with witches in 1692, he did not meddle. At seventy-six, he had fought enough battles.

Then in June, Constable Peter Osgood stopped by, asking after Higginson's daughter. Ann sat at her wheel, spinning. To Higginson's shock and horror, Osgood arrested her for using witchcraft against two Salem Village girls, Mary Walcott and Susanna Sheldon, and took her away. Speechless, he offered no resistance.

Ann's life had been a constant source of consternation since the day she married William Dolliver, a ne'er-do-well Gloucester sea captain. He had squandered most of her money and then taken off, leaving her alone to tend the children. Higginson was having his own problems collecting back pay from the church, but he took her and the children in. To cover the cost of feeding and clothing them, he had petitioned the courts to remove her remaining assets from her husband's control.

Under questioning, she would admit to curious behavior—staying out all night, either because she had lost her way or felt too faint to make it home. She hinted at family disputes, including disagreements with her stepmother, Higginson's new wife. The afflicted girls shamelessly accused Ann of pressing the life out of a child and of even trying to kill her own elderly father, "for she had more spite at him than she had at the child."

Her troubles had seized her with "overbearing melancholy" and left her "crazed in her understanding." That much Higginson acknowledged. He feared what the magistrates might induce her to say. She did admit that about fourteen years before, she had felt pinched, as if by evil spirits. She had consulted a book, which recommended wax poppets as a countermeasure. She had obtained two of them, though she swore she would never practice witchcraft "with intent to hurt anybody." Her revelations seemed to subdue the girls.

Ann would later be released. Higginson himself would derive comfort in the knowledge that very few of his fellow clerics approved of the witch trials, with the exception of his deluded assistant minister, Nicholas Noyes.

By 1696 the town owed him four hundred pounds, about five years' salary. His daughter had moved back in, and his expenses were piling up. Rather than antagonize the selectmen by demanding the back pay in a lump sum, he suggested they repay it in installments, for his daughter's maintenance. He and his wife, he knew, were not long for this world. Ann, on the other hand, had no means of income and still suffered severe bouts of melancholy.

To his relief, the selectmen consented. After his death in 1708, she would board in Rehoboth with Edward and Sarah Bishop, a Salem Village couple who had also survived the witch trials. The town paid her annual maintenance directly to the Bishops, an arrangement that proved satisfactory until 1723, when they found her too difficult to handle. By then, Reverend John Higginson was past worrying.

DEODAT LAWSON, SCITUATE, 50S

After George Burroughs resigned in 1683, Salem Village was without a minister. Then in August, the villagers called on Deodat Lawson, asking if he would serve on a trial basis.

A quiet, cheerless sort, he probably welcomed the invitation. Though a member of Boston's Second Church, Lawson had struck out in the pastoral department. He had been struggling with odd jobs to support his wife, Jane, and their two children. The truth was, he may not have been pastor material, yet his parents had insisted.

His father, a Puritan minister in England, had suffered persecution after the monarchy's restoration. Determined that his son follow in his footsteps, he had scraped together the resources to send him to college. (The name Deodat is taken from the Latin word *Adeodatus*, or "God given.") After six years of religious study, Deodat joined the stream of Puritans immigrating to Massachusetts, preaching initially at Martha's Vineyard.

Salem Village's invitation offered hope of a permanent appointment. Yet the community was fractious. After three years of rancorous negotiations, they offered him the job, but at this late stage, his enthusiasm had flagged. Four parishioners opposed him. So in the winter of 1687, Lawson signed on as chaplain for a military expedition to Maine led by the new London-appointed governor, Sir Edmund Andros. Soon after his return, his wife and daughter died. Grief-stricken, Lawson learned that certain villagers felt his tragic loss a fitting rebuke to a man who would abandon his flock over the winter.

Infuriated, he packed his bags and moved to Boston, where he took work at Boston's First Church before becoming the pastor of Scituate, Massachusetts, a post he held until 1698. Remarried now, he returned to the Salem Village parsonage in March of 1692 to inquire into the witchcraft outbreak. His observations, published in a ten-page pamphlet called *A Brief and True Narrative of Some Remarkable Passages Relating to Sundry Persons Afflicted by Witchcraft at Salem Village,* offered a valuable firsthand look at the episode, even if filtered through the uncritical eyes of a credulous outsider.

COTTON MATHER, BOSTON, 29

No one was surprised at the news that he was brilliant, a child prodigy certain to perpetuate the family's distinction. He cut his teeth on the Scriptures, praying as soon as he was old enough to talk. At the age of three, after recovering from a serious illness, he would say to his worried father, "Ton [Cotton] would go see God." By the time he was seven, he was composing prayers for his playmates, sometimes bullying them into reciting them. In adulthood he would regret it, remembering how they had taunted and punched him.

Cotton Mather, who more than anyone has come to symbolize the grim Puritanism of early New England, led a life of mental anguish. Guilt, self-loathing, shame, and a constant quest to win others' approval were just a few of the demons that fueled his florid obsessions.

His brilliant father, Increase Mather, was Boston's most distinguished preacher, a strict disciplinarian who raised his first child in a brooding atmosphere of fasting and self-reproach. From the start, Cotton was groomed for the ministry, relentlessly pressured to meet his father's lofty expectations. Cotton's grandfathers—John Cotton and Richard Mather—were among the most respected names in the colony's history. In appearance, he would take after the Cotton side of the family, dark-featured with a round face, a prominent nose, and a double chin. His father was purely Mather, long-faced with a high forehead and dour aspect.

With such enormous shoes to fill, Cotton drove himself to excess. From the esteemed Boston schoolmaster
Ezekiel Cheever, he would learn Greek, Hebrew, and
Latin. At age eleven and a half, he would enroll at Harvard, at a time when most first-year students were at
least fifteen. By the time he was fifteen, he had already
graduated, the youngest in the college's history.

He delivered his first sermon at sixteen and
earned a master's degree three years later. Cotton was
a shoe-in to succeed his father at the Second Church,
becoming an assistant there in 1683, when he was
barely twenty. His father, now the church's "teacher,"
would ordain him and share the pulpit. But there was
a price for such rapid ascendancy. In his early teens,
Cotton developed a stutter. Despairing of his future in
the ministry, he turned to the study of science and
medicine until a schoolmaster insisted he could lick
the problem if he would just speak slowly. The advice
seemed to work.

In 1680, the year he began to preach, Cotton
started a diary. He would tend it faithfully for the rest
of his life, while producing a prodigious number of sermons, pamphlets, and books. To read the entries is to
comprehend how central God was to his every per-
ception. Good days filled him with delirious joy that
his soul might be saved, while bad days threw him
into the depths of "darkness, horror, and confusion."
From a modern perspective, the two extremes suggest
bipolar disorder. At one end, he is euphorically visited
by angels; at the other, he is overcome by the darkest
"melancholy."

The pages of his lavishly worded journal overflow with veneration for his father. More than a family patriarch, the senior Mather was a spiritual force, all the more reason that Cotton struggled with a sense of inadequacy. Just as God issued messages by means of comets and rainbows, Cotton studied his father's actions for signs of approval or displeasure.

In 1681, hoping for a sign of affection, Cotton bought his father a "Spanish Indian" slave. Years later, when Cotton would receive a similar gift slave in return for a favor, he took it as a sign that "the Lord has most notably retaliated my dutifulness unto my father." His emotional needs would find unfortunate expression a decade later.

In 1686 Cotton married Abigail Phillips, the fifteen-year-old daughter of a wealthy Dorchester merchant. She bore nine children in six years but died in 1702. After a year in mourning, he married the widowed Elizabeth Hubbard. This marriage would last ten years and yield six children. He would have no children with his last wife, the widowed Lydia George, who struggled with mental illness but outlived him by six years. Of his fifteen children, six would live to adulthood, but only two, Nancy by his first wife and Samuel by his second, would still be alive at the time of his death in 1728, at the age of sixty-five.

He found solace in his work. During Sir Edmund Andros's despised rule in the 1680s, Cotton and his father led an underground campaign to oust him. While Increase was in London trying to procure a new charter, his son feverishly ministered to the flock, teaching, comforting the sick, calling on parishioners, delivering sermons, and presiding at funerals and executions. When Andros was overthrown, Cotton quickly mustered documents proclaiming the colony's right to independence.

But Boston's autonomy and economic prosperity had their downsides: Church membership was declining. People were drifting away from the religious teachings of the founding fathers. In part to lure them back, and in part because he feared apocalypse at the millennium's end, Cotton set to work on what would become one of the most influential of his nearly four hundred fifty works, *Memorable Providences Relating to Witchcrafts and Possessions.*

It examined the Goodwin family of Boston. In 1688, four of their six children were strangely bewitched by the mother of the family's Irish maidservant. An Irish Catholic, she confessed to the crime and was duly hanged. Through prayers and fasting, Cotton had helped the teenage sufferers recover from their fits, which lingered despite the matron's death. His message was unmistakable: Witches were a pernicious threat, but they would inevitably be unmasked and destroyed.

Three years after its publication, the witchcraft hysteria descended on Salem. Cotton kept his distance from the furor. With his father in London, he carried the entire burden of church affairs on his shoulders; he had caught a cold that he couldn't seem to shake. But he couldn't help but wonder. Salem's afflicted girls were behaving in ways suspiciously similar to the

Goodwin children, whose torments he had meticulously chronicled in his book. In late spring he would suggest that he take the Salem girls into his home for prayers and observation, as he had with Martha Goodwin, but his offer was declined. He would not attend the trials or even set foot in Salem except to watch the August 19 execution of Reverend George Burroughs. According to Boston merchant Robert Calef, Cotton's book about the Goodwins kindled the flames of the Salem witch hunt, thereby threatening "the destruction of the country."

Fearful that the devil was literally assaulting New England, and that he himself might die, Cotton fasted once a week, praying to God for protection against "the malice and power of the evil Angels."

As the news reached him that the court was convicting defendants based on tenuous "spectral" evidence, Cotton grew uneasy. Salem was a "thorny affair," he would write, but he would not own up to the court's errors until it was too late, and then only in writing. The trial judges, after all, were close associates whom he esteemed and admired. To some, he owed favors. And many were members of the government that had just been formed under the new charter, which his father had fought so hard to obtain. Governor Phips, who had appointed the justices to the witch court, was "one of my own Flock, and one of my dearest Friends." How could he question their judgment?

Instead, he wrote them letters vindicating them for their work. In an agitated missive to Salem judge John Richards, he speculated that the uproar might in fact signal the approach of the Second Coming, when Christ would set devils loose upon the earth. Privately, he was mystified by the whole affair. Over the course of the crisis, he would swing back and forth in his statements, defending the judges and then warning them away from spectral evidence, all the while apprehensive of speaking too hastily.

In 1693, when the proceedings were winding down, Abigail gave birth to a boy. At first he appeared to be healthy, but his intestines seemed strangely blocked. The doctor could make no sense of it, and three days later, the child died. Cotton attended the autopsy, noting the boy's lack of a "postern for the voidance of excrements." It was all so disturbing that he found "great reason to suspect a witchcraft in this preternatural accident." Rumors circulated that his wife had given birth to a monster. She must be a witch. But with the trials nearly over, the matter was dropped.

In the midst of it, two witchcraft cases fell into his lap. A pair of seventeen-year-old Boston girls, Mercy Short and then Margaret Rule, started experiencing fits. He took Mercy into his home, in what would turn into a community-wide attempt to exorcise the evil spirits possessing her. Mercy would recover, though he had less success with Margaret.

Robert Calef, suspicious of his intentions, accused him of sexual improprieties with the girl, an assertion that so enraged the younger Mather that he sued the Boston merchant for slander, a suit he later would drop. But with his detailed notes, Cotton described his efforts with the girls in two published pamphlets,

A Brand Pluck'd Out of the Burning and *Another Brand Pluckt Out of the Burning.*

Only in 1696 would Cotton Mather concede that the witch trials had been a mistake. In December, as the colony contemplated its problems, a group of ministers asked him to draft an official proclamation explaining the cause of its troubles. Included in the list was "the late inexplicable storms from the Invisible World," namely the Salem witchcraft events, whereby "we were lead into errors and great hardships were brought upon innocent persons and (we fear) guilt incurred, which we all have cause to bewail with much confusion of face before the Lord."

In his 1699 monograph, *Decennium Luctuosum,* he used the colony's second Indian conflict, King William's War, as a metaphor in describing the Salem witchcraft struggle, placing blame on warring tribes. "I have met with some strange things, not here to me mentioned," he wrote, "which have made me often think that this inexplicable war might have some of its original among the Indians, whose chief sagamores are well known unto some of our captives to have been horrid sorcerers, and hellish conjurers, and such as conversed with demons."

Ultimately, public respect for Cotton Mather was starting to wane. He had chronicled the Salem witch trials in a book titled *Wonders of the Invisible World,* which defended the court's actions. He came close to the Harvard presidency in 1701, when his father was removed and his name was submitted as a successor. But the college nixed it, though it was the one office he most desired. Then in 1702, he undertook what would become his major opus, *Magnalia Christi Americanais,* a history of the Massachusetts Colony.

Perhaps his greatest legacy would be scientific. Smallpox epidemics continued to sweep through Boston, leaving death and misery. In 1706 an African slave explained how he had managed to stay immune to the dreaded disease. As a child in Africa, the slave had been inoculated. Cotton passed the news on to Boston's physicians, who scoffed at the notion. But one of them was curious enough to give it a try. Dr. Zabdiel Boylston inoculated two slaves, an adult and a child, and his only son. All three recovered. Their success inspired death threats. Cotton hid Boylston in his home and avoided going out for fear of attack. A bomb was even lobbed into his house.

For years afterward, he would continue to contemplate God's purpose in sending witchcraft upon the people. He would even exhort the government to make amends to the victims' families. Clearly he had come to regret the trials and realize that he had been wrong about them. Yet unlike Samuel Sewall, Mather would never go public with an apology.

Neither would he ever match his father's success. Only by surviving Increase Mather in 1723 would he take command of the Second Church, but even that triumph would be short-lived. Within five years, Cotton Mather was dead.

INCREASE MATHER, BOSTON, 53

Nightmares plagued him most of his life. Increase Mather, one of America's greatest seventeenth-century clerics, might have been intellectually and diplomatically gifted, but he was acutely unsuited to the task of nurturing a congregation.

His brilliant father, Reverend Richard Mather, had fled English persecution and settled in Dorchester, Massachusetts, where he would preach for almost thirty-four years. His first wife, Katherine Mather, had given him six sons, five of whom survived into adulthood. Increase, the youngest, would become a respected Boston divine, as reserved as he was intellectual.

According to Cotton Mather, Increase's unusual Christian name was conferred upon him in reference to the "never-to-be-forgotten increase, of every sort, wherewith God favoured the country." At the time of his birth in 1639, the Great Migration was under way, with Puritan families fleeing England in droves for a better life in the colonies. His father would teach Increase Greek and Latin, and at the age of twelve, he would enroll at Harvard to study for the ministry. By his own admission, Increase had a "weak constitution of Body." Concerned about his health, his father took him out of Harvard for a time and put him under the care of a close friend, the scholarly John Norton. Each week Norton took Increase and his other student boarders to Boston's First Church, exposing them early in life to the city's largest and most upscale congregation.

At the age of fifteen, Increase would fall ill from what he termed "the stone," resulting in slow, painful urination. Like the nightmares, the affliction would beset him most of his life. More debilitating still was his melancholy. His mother's death in 1655 caused him such distress that he experienced a religious conversion. By his eighteenth birthday, he had matured enough to deliver his first sermon. Soon he would preach from his father's Dorchester pulpit, just as his own son, Cotton Mather, would one day preach from his.

Obviously, religion was in the Mather wiring. Five of Increase's six brothers would join the ministry. The two eldest, Nathaniel and Samuel, pursued preaching careers in England. Samuel, a Senior Fellow at Trinity College in Dublin, suggested that Increase enroll there to do his master of arts degree. Increase had graduated from Harvard, so with his father's permission, he set sail. Conditions in England had improved: The monarchy was gone, Oliver Cromwell's Puritan government ruled the land, and many Harvard graduates were sailing back.

He arrived in Dublin in 1657. Within months he caught the measles, then a slight case of smallpox. But he enrolled nonetheless, completing his degree in 1658. Eager to escape Ireland's chilly dampness, he moved to London, where Cromwell's personal chaplain, John Howe, offered him the pastorate at Great Torrington, a Devon town only nine miles from the home of Increase's brother Nathaniel.

The arrangement seemed ideal. Increase gratefully accepted the position that winter, but by September, everything was off. Oliver Cromwell had died, and so had the Puritan experiment. Howe now needed his old pastorate back, so Increase was forced to move out. Nathaniel's father-in-law managed to find him a post as chaplain with an English garrison on the Isle of Guernsey, a bleak and isolated outpost.

But following King Charles II's coronation in 1661, a popular backlash began sweeping Puritans out of England's churches. Increase's brother Nathaniel lost his ministry in Barnstable, and Samuel was removed from his positions in Dublin. In Guernsey, Increase was told to cast off Puritanism and embrace Anglican beliefs. He refused. In his autobiography, he proudly describes refusing to drink to the king's health and refusing to subscribe to the belief that with the end of Puritan rule, times "would be happy." His preaching had won accolades; he could have earned four hundred pounds per year, he wrote, if he would only conform to the Church of England. He would not.

As the year wore on, Congregationalists began to flee. Nathaniel found a position in the Netherlands. Increase intended to follow him there with a friend, but when the friend backed down, the only rational option was Boston.

Puritan rule may have ended in England, but it was still alive in the American colonies. Increase "wept for Joy" at the sight of his father, and indeed, his father nearly broke down upon seeing his erudite son preaching from the pulpit. At twenty-two, Increase was suddenly in high demand; he had experienced religious persecution like the greatest Puritan leaders. At least a dozen congregations invited him to preach. After a two-year delay, he would settle on the Old North meetinghouse, later known as Boston's Second Church.

Committing to a Boston congregation proved difficult. He had taken a liking to English life and hoped to return. Ordination would mean a lifelong commitment to the New World, where libraries and scholarship were scarce. He lacked the patience to act the peacemaker, or to prod the congregation to pay his salary, as other pastors did. Reluctantly, he accepted the church's invitation but left himself an out: Should he fall ill or feel persecuted, underpaid, or called to greater service, he would be free to go.

As his ordination approached, he felt "grieved, grieved, grieved, with temptations to Atheism." His father would assist at the 1664 ceremony, yet for three years, Increase would experience bitter discontent over his miniscule pay, the congregation's lack of proper deference, and his general displeasure at being in Boston. His financial difficulties wouldn't ease until later, when the church gained some wealthy members who bolstered his salary.

The raise came just in time, as his family obligations were growing. Seven months after his return, he married Maria Cotton, which posed another problem: Living in her father's house on a hill overlooking Boston, it took an hour to walk to church. During his absence, his father had married Maria's mother, the widow of the famous Reverend John Cotton. By marrying Maria, his own stepsister, Increase consciously enhanced his theological qualifications and prestige. After all, his family represented two of the colony's most respected names.

The first of their ten children, Cotton, was born a year later. Increase would prove a devoted father, but unfortunately for his family, a reclusive one.

He spent sixteen-hour days secluded in his study, emerging only to eat and sleep, leaving Maria to manage the household affairs. He discouraged visitors, preferring to immerse himself in contemplation and intellectual pursuits. At first Maria balked, complaining on one occasion that while she always focused on his good qualities, he only took notice of her faults. Soon after, she tearfully demanded that he move out, seeing as he was so mercilessly critical of Boston.

It probably didn't help that Increase's mother-in-law was a frequent guest, discussing him as the two women did their chores. As ministers' wives, they were burdened by a double load of domestic and religious obligations. Six times a day, they put their work aside to pray. Once and sometimes twice a year, they were required to read the Bible from start to finish. They could perform virtually no chores at all on the Sabbath, but they had to dress modestly, show humility and self-effacement, demonstrate utter obedience, and be charitable to the poor. Years later, Increase would praise Maria for her piety, self-sacrifice, and the trouble she took to never displease him.

His solitude was indispensable, as it opened his mind, he felt, to mystical intuition. At least once he sensed himself immersed in thoughts of heaven; a few days later he discovered that at that very moment, his brother Eleazer had died. At other times he felt as if he had communed with God or sensed premonitions of his own impending death. His sermons were sprinkled with subtle death wishes, yet Increase Mather would live to be eighty-four.

His father would not. In April of 1669, at seventy-three, Richard Mather fell ill at Increase's home and died a week later. That fall, Increase had a nervous breakdown. His depression would prove so debilitating that he was unable to preach or even leave the house. In the spring of 1671, he developed nightmares so severe that he feared he was going insane. Leaving Maria at home with the four children, he lodged for several weeks at a mineral springs in Lynn, Massachusetts, believing that depression and hypochondria were a function of the spleen and that they might be cured with the proper treatment.

The recurrent nightmares eased, but he would never be rid of them completely. That same year, the Mathers moved into a new house in Boston's North End, a busy, elegant part of town with coffeehouses and shops.[5] Though physically closer to the church, he remained psychologically distant from his flock. Some displayed little sympathy for his nervous disorder, and Increase, now with five children and a growing debt, desired nothing more than to leave for England.

When he realized that his eldest son, Cotton, was cursed with a stammer, he called his wife and child into his study to pray, to tearfully confess their sinfulness, and to beg God's mercy. It was in his study that Increase memorized lectures and sermons so that he could deliver them on the Sabbath without notes. He wrote daily in his diary; during his lifetime he penned over 125 books and pamphlets.

Gradually he was becoming Boston's most prominent preacher and New England's leading scholar, whose writings made him famous on both sides of the Atlantic. He would chronicle the first Indian War in 1676, a violent year that ended with untold bloodshed. That November, fire swallowed up about eighty houses in Boston's North End, including his own. Despite a cold drizzle, the house burst into flames just before dawn. Increase bundled Maria and the younger children onto the street, then scrambled back in to save his thousand-tome library. He piled the most important volumes onto thirteen-year-old Cotton's outstretched arms, sent him out, then started throwing books down the stairs. Neighbors salvaged linens and furniture, but the heavier pieces could not be moved. The North Church also burned. "This," Increase wrote, "was the Fatal and dismall day."

The church would be rebuilt, bigger and better than before. The Mathers would spend 1677 in a leased house, but Maria's mother had died the year before, and the sale of her house had yielded enough for her and Increase to build a home near the church. This one would belong to them alone.

Yet it wasn't until the following year that political events induced Increase Mather to step onto the political stage. While respecting the English monarchy, Massachusetts considered itself a self-governing colony by virtue of its signed and sealed charter. So when King James II revoked the document and sent Royal Governor Edmund Andros to take over the reins, it was a slap in the face.

Increase actively worked to build opposition to this royal intrusion, publishing protests and organizing underground meetings. When that failed, he disguised himself and secretly boarded ship, arriving in London in 1688 to try his hand at personal persuasion. As it happened, James II was overthrown during his visit, forcing him to start anew with the monarch's successor, William III. Unlike the Catholic James, King William was Protestant and eager to oblige. In 1692 Increase returned to Boston a hero. His new charter was better in many respects than the one it replaced. It established an elected legislature, enfranchised all male landowners instead of solely male church members, and united Massachusetts with Plymouth Colony. In June of that year, Increase was appointed president of Harvard College.

But in Salem, the witch trials were in full swing. Despite Increase's private misgivings, his son Cotton had risen to become his assistant at the church. Though a brilliant young man and avid learner, on matters of witchcraft, Increase felt, Cotton was out of his depth. In public, Increase denied that they differed on the matter, but in fact, they did. While Cotton fueled the frenzy with vitriolic statements, Increase observed the trials and visited with the suspects in jail. A few of them confessed to the witchcraft charges that had been hurled against them, but many recanted, saying they had confessed under coercion, and that they regretted their lies. In August he met in Cambridge with seven other Boston-area ministers, most of whom revealed grave misgivings about the witch trials.

He continued to preach vigilance. In September, he published *Cases of Conscience concerning evil Spirits,*[6] an essay voicing support for the trials' premise, but denouncing spectral evidence as unreliable, and questioning the credibility of the accusers and even of the confessed witches themselves.

It was as strident as his criticism would get. In the trials' aftermath, a Boston businessman, Robert Calef, would attack Increase for not doing more to stop the proceedings. Calef's book, *More Wonders of the Invisible World,* so offended the elder Mather that in 1700 he ordered it burned.

When the storm had passed, Increase Mather woke up to a changed world. The Mather name now tarnished, he watched his influence shrivel. When Harvard insisted that he move closer to Cambridge, he resigned the presidency. He ventured less often into the political arena, focusing instead on his own writing and social engagements. As always, he was quick to meet with the erudite and wealthy but neglected the humbler members of his flock.

He would try in vain to mend the hopeless chasm that had divided Samuel Parris from his Salem Village congregation, eventually suggesting that Parris leave. Parris rejected his advice. Increase never openly condemned the judges, most of whom were close friends. Nor did he voice regret that he had not done more to prevent the damage done to the trial victims. Instead he withdrew into his own private realm. His son Cotton being active in the church, he was freed for more contemplative preoccupations. Perhaps he intuited that the Puritan era was closing.

His wife, Maria, would die in 1714. A year later he married Ann Lake, effectively replacing one Cotton descendent with another. While Maria had been the daughter of the esteemed Reverend John Cotton, Ann was his grandson's widow.

He fainted one day in 1722 and was virtually bedridden until his death from bladder failure a year later. Interred in the Mather tomb on Copp's Hill, he became—like the door-shaped gravestone above him—a weathered monument to former glory, his life achievements diminished under the weight of an epic disgrace.

JOSHUA MOODY, BOSTON, 59

Most Puritan ministers were hesitant to unleash their criticism on any but the lowliest members of their flock. Joshua Moody did not differentiate. His refusal to cast a blind eye at the transgressions of the wealthy and powerful would earn him the highest respect but also cause him anguish.

He was born to William Moody, an illiterate saddler. In about 1634, when Joshua was barely a year old, the family moved from Ipswich in England to Ipswich in Massachusetts. Joshua was schooled in Newbury, probably by the local parson, Reverend Thomas Parker, who may have steered him toward the ministry. Joshua entered Harvard in 1655, joining the Cambridge church.

After graduation in 1658, Moodey (as he spelled it) started preaching in Portsmouth, New Hampshire, where he was formally invited to stay on in 1660. Two years later, to demonstrate how seriously they took their faith, the villagers installed an outdoor cage as public humiliation for those "such as sleepe or take tobacco on the Lord's day out of the meeting in the time of the publique exercise."

It was a revealing sign of Moody's fervor. In 1671 his fledgling church boasted a mere nine members, but it was no less devout. One of Moody's first tasks was to raise sixty pounds to replace the ramshackle wooden school with a brick one, pleased that the little village could make do for itself without begging for Boston's help.

But in 1682, his parishioners seized a Scottish ketch for "breach of the revenue laws," probably failing to pay customs duties. The vessel's owner, one of Moody's flock, claimed he knew nothing of any violation, but in court that December, it was clear that he had lied. A private discussion between him and the governor and duty collector seemed to clear the matter up, but Moody smelled a rat. He wrote to the governor's office and asked to see the documents, citing the need for church discipline. His request was refused.

The lieutenant governor, Edward Cranfield, insisted that the man had been forgiven. Further meddling was inadvisable, he exclaimed, and if Moody pursued the case, he would regret it.

At the meetinghouse, the reverend delivered a sermon about the dangers of lying. The congregation then decided to confront the duty evader and seek his confession. Enraged, Cranfield issued an order. Starting in January, any minister refusing to administer the Anglican sacraments would be punished. He then sent an officer to Moody's house to inform him that he and four others intended to take communion that Sunday, the Anglican way. Moody declined and sent the envoy away. The following Saturday, Moody received a summons demanding that he appear in Boston that Monday. When he showed up, he was arrested.

In court, Moody explained that he had declined the officer's request as he was not trained in the Episcopal faith, nor paid to preach it. He then reminded the justices that the whole purpose of settling New England was to be free from such arbitrary laws. They disagreed. Moody was given six months without bail. He asked to see the governor but was refused. The authorities did consent to let him serve out his term in virtual house arrest, at the home of a sea captain, Elias Stileman. He was confined to his room in the captain's house on Great Island, a sandy peninsula extending several miles south into Cape Cod Bay. Forbidden to preach or to pray with anyone other than the Stilemans, Moody sent a letter to a former Harvard classmate, Reverend Samuel Phillips. After Lieutenant Governor Cranfield had left for New York on business, the meetinghouse was quietly reopened; Phillips came to lead the service. Moody was allowed a visit home to see his family. His friends later intervened on his behalf, and he was released after thirteen weeks but forbidden to preach.

Cotton Mather would later praise him as the first to suffer "for that Cause [religious persecution] in these parts of the World." But Cranfield's grudge was more personal than philosophical, and Moody knew it. So in the spring of 1684, the minister traveled to Boston and approached the prestigious First Church, which voted to offer him a position assisting the Reverend James Allen.

Two months later, Harvard offered Moody its presidency, which he declined. His heart was still in Portsmouth. He would return frequently to the seaside community after 1685, the year Cranfield was removed from office together with the despotic Edmund Andros. Moody was becoming one of a select group of Boston ministers whose influence spilled into politics and the judiciary. Andros's deputy, Edward

Randolph, would catch a glimpse of him at Andros's ouster, sitting in the government chambers.

By 1692 Moody was seriously mulling the prospect of returning to Portsmouth when Salem's prisons started filling up with accused witches. Though he never publicly expressed his views on the trials, he would in private, and obliquely, through his choice of biblical texts. In May, for example, he delivered the Election Day sermon in Boston. For his text he quoted the prophet Samuel's speech to his followers, in which Samuel reminds them of God's blessings and then scolds them for putting greater trust in earthly kings than in God.

Then in August, Moody and a like-minded minister, Samuel Willard, paid a visit to the Boston jail keeper's house to console the wealthy Philip and Mary English of Salem, who were incarcerated there on charges of witchcraft. Later, as their trial date approached, he met the couple there and accompanied them to the First Church, where he preached a sermon drawn from Matthew 10:23. "But when they persecute you in this city, flee ye into another." The Englishes took the hint, escaping to New York until the panic blew over.

The extent to which Moody engineered their escape is unclear. That he assisted them is likely, as Willard's son had helped another prominent couple, Captain Nathaniel Cary and his accused wife, Elizabeth. That summer, as if intuiting Moody's opposition to the witch trials, a rumor made the rounds that the reverend's wife, Ann Jacobs Moody, was also among the guilty.

Nothing came of it, but the family was happy to leave Boston the following year and return to their beloved Portsmouth. Moody would remain active there until the winter of 1695, when Ann was struck with palsy, leaving her unable to talk and paralyzed in her right side. Then in 1697, Moody himself took sick. He traveled to Boston to consult a doctor and died there, aged sixty-five, near the King's Chapel Burying Ground.

He had wanted to be buried by his first wife, Martha Collins. She had died in 1674, along with several of their children. But it being July, his body could not be kept, so he was interred in Boston in the tomb of John Hull, the Boston merchant, mintmaster, and cofounder both of Harvard College and the Third Church. A great crowd turned out at his funeral, despite his articulated wish that efforts be made to strictly inhibit "those profuse expenses in mourning, or otherwise so frequently wasted at funerals." Cotton Mather gave the eulogy. Joshua Moody was mourned by four children and two New England congregations.

Nicholas Noyes, Salem, 45

He was an odd man, stout of figure, a lifelong bachelor who enjoyed lively dinner conversation and wrote
an occasional line of verse. As the deputy minister, or
"teacher," in bustling Salem, he had been working for
nine years under the direction of the Reverend John
Higginson, who at seventy-six was still venerated, but
slowing down. Noyes had graduated from Harvard in
the class of 1667. During King Philip's War, he went to
Maine as chaplain for the English troops fighting the
Indians. If there was one thing the experience taught
him, it was that evil could rise up in material form, and
that when it did, it must be rooted out and destroyed.

That revelation was not forgotten when demonic
spirits descended upon Massachusetts in 1692. Once
again, Noyes volunteered his services, this time as
the official chaplain at the Salem witchcraft trials. His
eagerness might have had something to do with his
long fascination with the book of Revelations. Perhaps
fearing that its dark prophecies were coming to pass, he
resolved to overpower the evil forces by urging the condemned to examine their souls and repent. But often
he behaved more like a judge than a preacher. Like the
presiding magistrates, Noyes openly questioned the
suspects' testimony and was quick to presume guilt.
When John Alden complained that the afflicted girls
were accusing innocent people, Noyes interrupted
him and talked on until Alden was silenced. During
Martha Corey's interrogation in March, he felt no com-
punctions about expressing his opinion. "I believe it is

apparent," he confidently asserted, that "she practis-
eth Witchcraft in the congregation."

He would live his entire life in the Province of
Massachusetts Bay, having been born in Newbury in
1647 and educated there and then at Harvard, where
he graduated with a degree in divinity two decades
later. He was a close friend and frequent dinner guest
at the home of witchcraft judge Samuel Sewall, who
had studied under the same blind Newbury schoolmaster, Thomas Parker, Noyes's great-uncle. He would
attend the proceedings—and the executions—often in
the company of Sewall and other dignitaries. After one
such execution on September 22, Noyes stood back to
observe the bodies of the women he had just ushered
into the next life, uttering a remark memorable for its
false empathy: "What a sad thing it is to see eight fire-
brands of Hell hanging there."

Yet even he would be hurt by the witchcraft scare.
His cousin, Sarah Noyes Hale, was accused of witchcraft.
The wife of the Beverly parson, John Hale, she was six
months pregnant at the time and of such exemplary
character that the charges were summarily dismissed.

He also had a chilling exchange with Sarah Good,
a beggar given the death sentence for refusing to
confess. Facing her as she stood at the gallows with
the noose about her neck, he hectored the innocent
woman, declaring that she was a witch, she knew it,
and that it was her last chance to admit it and clear
herself. "Liar!" she shouted. "I am no more a witch
than you are a wizard, and if you take away my life,
God will give you blood to drink."

He stayed on as assistant minister after the trials were over, but gradually came to regret the witch hunt, as it had sullied his reputation. In his writings on the episode, Boston merchant Thomas Brattle ridiculed him for being so gullible. Later, when a group of ministers drew up a petition requesting that the afflicted girls be pardoned for their misbehavior, Noyes demonstrated his change of heart by refusing to sign.

But twenty-six years later, Sarah Good's prophecy came to pass. In 1718, at the age of seventy, Noyes suffered a brain hemorrhage and very likely choked on his own blood.

SAMUEL PARRIS, SALEM VILLAGE, 39

A failed businessman, Samuel Parris would fare no better in the ministry. He consistently placed his own personal interests over those of his parish, even when it resulted in the loss of innocent lives.

Born to a London cloth merchant, he sailed to Boston in the 1660s and studied at Harvard. Upon his father's death in 1673, he dropped out of school and traveled to Barbados to collect his inheritance, including a sugar plantation his father had owned.

Now a merchant, after eight years he returned to Boston and continued his trading business, now with a family and three slaves, including Tituba and John Indian. To bolster his prestige, he began preaching at local churches, and after a long period of negotiation, accepted the Salem Village (Danvers) pulpit in 1689.

At first the congregation was impressed with his religious orthodoxy, but gradually they soured on him. He was rough with his slaves and openly self-serving, and though they paid him a decent salary and all his firewood, he demanded more. Parris exuded a sense of entitlement, insisting that he own the title to the parsonage, though such an arrangement would be disadvantageous to the parish. The village had already seen three other preachers come and go; if Parris were to leave as quickly as his predecessors, the home would be lost.

As time passed, the dispute deepened, dividing the village into two factions. The more conservative sided with Parris, while the more prosperous opposed him. By October of 1691, his opponents had stopped contributing their shares to his salary, and the rift was festering. Parris, consumed with worry over his financial debts, his wife in bed sick, his food running low, and his firewood almost gone, was at an emotional impasse. Then in February of 1692, his daughter Betty and his orphaned niece, Abigail Williams, started acting oddly.

They threw embers around the room, barked like dogs, crawled under furniture, and convulsed, as if epileptic. The doctor was called but could find nothing wrong with them, finally concluding they were suffering from diabolic possession. The minister, appalled to have such activities going on in the parsonage, urged the girls to tell him who was responsible. Abigail named the slave Tituba, so he turned his attention there. She denied involvement. Some historians contend that he beat it out of her.

By now the hysteria had spread to neighboring households, and Parris was the center of attention. Ministers and dignitaries stopped in to observe the girls' condition. In one sense, the witchcraft might have been a welcome distraction. The community, overwhelmed by an emergency, temporarily ceased its griping and bonded together. He would send his daughter Betty to Salem Town, where she would be able to convalesce away from the uproar, and concentrated on recording the trials and interrogations. Much of what is known about the proceedings comes from his longhand notes. Later, most of the parish records mysteriously disappeared.

When the crisis blew over, his slave Tituba was still in prison, but Parris refused to pay the fees to enable her release. Instead, she was sold to an unknown slave trader. He preached each Sunday as before, but church attendance continued to dwindle. His congregation had not forgotten the sermons he had delivered in the spring of 1692, calling for swift convictions. His opponents would form a solid faction and campaign for his dismissal. They had long stopped paying their share of his salary and became more vocal in their opposition to his ownership of the parsonage. In 1695 a group of Massachusetts clergymen convened in Salem to sort the conflict out, but to no avail.

The beleaguered pastor clung to the pulpit, probably fearful of finding an appointment elsewhere. A few times he extended a peace offering; in one sermon he encouraged "kisses" among friends. Yet he scolded his congregation for the "lies" they spread about him, and even threatened litigation. But as he asked their forgiveness "wherein you see or conceive I have erred or offended," he would never apologize or even acknowledge his role in fueling the witch hunt.

In 1697, after a four-year battle, Parris resigned. He would refuse to vacate the parsonage until he had collected his back pay, then accepted a preaching invitation in Stow. He moved three times more, first to Concord, then to Dunstable, and finally to Sudbury, where he died in 1720 at age sixty-seven.

As it happened, his daughter Betty would fare better in life than her afflicted friends. She married and settled in Concord, Massachusetts, where she raised five children and lived to be seventy-seven. Parris's son Noyes, on the other hand, would die insane.

SAMUEL WILLARD, 52, BOSTON

He had seen it all before. In the winter of 1671, when he was preaching in Groton, Massachusetts, one of his own maidservants had spent three months in a state of diabolical possession. Now it was happening all over again in Salem Village.

Samuel Willard would never forget it. Elizabeth Knapp, a young woman of sixteen, had swooned and convulsed, shrieking at the top of her lungs and then falling silent, as if struck from behind. She accused a neighbor of bewitching her, but he had deliberately ignored it, urging her instead to pray. Her speech had been so scattered and contradictory that he knew that the wisest action was to withhold judgment.

At one point she had confessed that the devil had deluded her, though he never truly believed she could have signed away her soul. She was more "an object of pity," as he would later write, than a lost spirit. He had never given up on her, and eventually, she had recovered.

How differently they were handling things now, twenty-one years later. Back then it had all been resolved without trials and executions. But Knapp's case differed from Salem's in one crucial point. The devil had actually inhabited Elizabeth Knapp, rather than just luring her into a diabolical pact. He wasn't sure what was wrong with her, but he had known enough to wait it out.

By contrast, the Salem trial judges—even Reverend Nicholas Noyes—seemed to believe every word the bewitched girls uttered.

From his pulpit at Boston's Third (South) Church, Willard urged compassion for the accused, but his pleas fell on deaf ears. Three of his parishioners, Samuel Sewall, Wait Winthrop, and Peter Sergeant, were all witch trial judges. It was within their power to question the proceedings, but they seemed as immune to his urgings as everyone else. Only Nathaniel Saltonstall, his old Harvard classmate, would have the sense to speak out.

Willard was a popular minister with a large congregation. He had preached at the Old South Church since 1678, having succeeded the eminent Thomas Thatcher. A year later he married Eunice Tyng, whose father, the magistrate Edward Tyng, was a friend of Reverend George Burroughs. It was his second marriage. His first, to Abigail Sherman, had ended with her death.

He had lived thirteen years in Groton, on the edge of the wilderness. In March of 1676, Indians raided the town, forcing its three hundred settlers to flee. The Willards migrated to Charlestown. Two years later, after delivering a few sermons at Boston's Third Church, he was hired as Thatcher's assistant. He would take over after Thatcher's death later that year. With the likes of John Hull, Thomas Brattle, and Samuel Sewall as members, his sermons were conscientiously intended, and usually heeded. To make sure his listeners grasped his message, Willard phrased it simply.

In May he confirmed Satan's existence, urging that his listeners "be sober, be vigilant, because your adversary the devil, as a roaring lion, walketh about seeking whom he may devour."

Then on June 19, he warned against giving false witness, as those who do so "are the devil's brokers." As usual, he saw that many in the congregation were taking notes, including Samuel Sewall and his merchant friend, Edward Bromfield. "The Devil may represent an innocent, nay a godly person, doing a bad act," Willard exclaimed, and as if by magic, take on "the image of any man in the world."

In July, after sea captain John Alden had been jailed, Willard attended a gathering at the man's house and led the prayer. Soon after, he addressed a letter to the Court of Oyer and Terminer, signed by the ministers of all three of Boston's churches, to protest Alden's incarceration. It drew no response, but Willard continued to call for compassion nonetheless.

As more innocents were swept away, including members of his own flock, he decided to actively intervene. Learning that Salem merchants Phillip and Mary English were detained in Boston prison, he and his assistant minister, Joshua Moody, invited them to a service. Moody preached from Matthew 10:23: "But when they persecute you in this city, flee ye into another." Later he paid them a visit to make sure they understood, explaining that "several worthy Persons in Boston" were ready to help them escape.

After one sermon, he had a scare. He had warned that the devil could impersonate perfectly innocent people, knowing that it would raise eyebrows, as the subtext was that the judges were condemning innocent people. He was not surprised to learn that soon after, one of the possessed girls had cried out in court that "Mr. Willard" was afflicting her. As Robert Calef noted, the judges ordered the girl out of the room, mumbling that she must have gotten her names mixed up. True, he wasn't the only Willard; there was John Willard, the former Salem constable who now stood accused of witchcraft, and Simon Willard, the minister's brother, a Salem clothier and veteran of the Maine Indian troubles who had testified against Reverend Burroughs.

But there was no mistake. The judges knew who the girl was referring to but chose to ignore it. They had complete trust in their pastor, even if his views diverged from their own. Willard toned down his sermons in the latter part of July, perhaps not wishing to press his luck. That fall, he put his concerns to paper and distributed them anonymously as a dialogue between S. and B., Salem and Boston. In it he professed the innocence of such people as Phillip English and John Alden. Thomas Brattle, another member of Willard's congregation, wrote his own angry denunciation of the trials that fall, as did Reverend Increase Mather.

Two years after the witch trials had ended, Willard's previous parish, where he had preached for thirteen years until the first Indian war made it impossible to remain, was destroyed. The warriors crept in at dawn in late July, unnoticed, and though a hundred mounted militiamen rushed in to aid his former flock, all they found was twenty corpses. The next night, Willard would bury his one-year-old daughter, Sarah.

By 1700, when Robert Calef's scathing condemnation of the witch trials had been published in London and made its way back to Boston, Willard was recovering from a bronchial flu that nearly killed him. He would die seven years later, at sixty-seven.

CHAPTER 4

THE JUDGES

The justices appointed to the Court of Oyer and Terminer were distinguished politicians drawn from the
General Court, the colony's governing body. All owed
their positions to family connections and years of public service, but also to the power derived from their own
personal wealth. Many had inherited their fortunes, but
when not sitting on the bench or advising the governor,
most if not all engaged in other enterprises. Wait Still
Winthrop and Bartholomew Gedney practiced medicine on the side. Winthrop drew a military salary, as
did Nathaniel Saltonstall. Samuel Sewall owned mills,
and Peter Sergeant's international trading had made
him the richest man in Boston. If they rendered public
service, it was by choice instead of need.

A tight-knit cabal, the judges socialized together,
intermarried, and collaborated on entrepreneurial
schemes. Between them, they held title to thousands
of New England acres, much of it wilderness property.
The majority was purchased for a song from Indians
left destitute between the two Indian conflicts, from
the 1678 end of King Philip's War to the start of King
William's War in 1688. Some of this prime real estate,
which stretched from the upper Maine coastline to the
tip of Rhode Island, was procured through dubious
government contracts.

With their fine suits and gabled mansions, they looked for all the world like English gentry. A few, like the wealthy John Richards, had started out humble. Land, they knew, was the only guaranteed ticket to long-term wealth. By the 1690s, two generations of English settlement had locked most Massachusetts property into private ownership. Even Cotton Mather lamented the land hunger that obsessed his friends and associates. Where once an acre had sufficed, then twenty to raise a family, now hundreds, "nay thousands of Acres, have been engrossed by one man," he would write, "and they that profess themselves Christians have forsaken Churches, and Ordinances, and all for land and elbow-room enough in the World."

Many of these wilderness investments would backfire in 1689, as settlers fled the frontier settlements to escape marauding Indians, abandoning the now worthless properties. Adding to the panic was the fact that the front was moving closer to Boston. A month before hysteria gripped Salem Village, some fifty settlers were massacred in York, Maine, including Samuel Sewall's cousin, the Reverend Shubael Dummer.

Those with the largest property holdings were probably Wait Winthrop and his brother-in-law, John Richards. Richards had purchased frontier land as far back as 1649, when he acquired Arrowsic Island on the southern coast of Maine from an Androscoggin sachem. Winthrop inherited thousands of remote acres in Connecticut, Rhode Island, and Massachusetts, adding more to his holdings in 1686, while serving under the Andros regime. Bartholomew Gedney owned a saw- and gristmill in what today is Yarmouth, Maine, and Jonathan Corwin had one in Wells. Even the high-principled Nathaniel Saltonstall, who would resign from the bench in protest, owned a tract in Connecticut and another along the Piscataqua River.

Samuel Sewall procured his wealth through marriage. His father-in-law, John Hull, bequeathed him Boston warehouses, ships, mills, and a substantial share of the Pettaquamscut Purchase, whose prominent shareholders speculated in Narragansett Indian territory in Rhode Island.[1] In 1687 Sewall traveled to Salmon Falls (now Berwick, Maine) to visit his sawmills, spending a night with his cousin Shubael. Over the years, Sewall invested an estimated two thousand pounds in his distant properties, only to have them torched by Indian raiders in 1689 and 1690. Until they were rebuilt, he suffered severe losses on his grain and lumber exports, while his colleagues found themselves weighed down by properties that they couldn't sell.

There was little any of them could do about it from Salem, unless it was to prosecute the occasional settler suspected of collaborating with the enemy. If not for Satan's minions, the thinking went, they wouldn't have suffered such financial losses. It was in that vein that the magistrates sympathized with the afflicted girls, especially the ones whose families had been slain on the Maine frontier. And it was for that reason that they vigorously punished suspected collaborators, like Reverend George Burroughs.

Governor Phips, fresh back from England and clueless about legal protocol, would appoint a special tribunal to handle the witchcraft cases. Officially, such ad hoc courts had to be sanctioned by the legislature, but considering the urgency, that detail was overlooked. The resulting commission, the Court of Oyer and Terminer, was probably illegal, but then, the entire court system had broken down in 1684 with the charter's abrogation; it would take years before it was reestablished.

Meanwhile, nine justices were appointed to try the cases; five would constitute a quorum, as long as either Stoughton, Richards, or Gedney were present. Stoughton, the lieutenant governor, would double as chief justice. The remaining eight—each of whom were respected politicians—included Nathaniel Saltonstall, Samuel Sewall, Wait Still Winthrop, John Richards, John Hathorne, Jonathan Corwin, Bartholomew Gedney, and Peter Sergeant.

It remains unclear which of the nine served at the court's various sessions, since in the trials' aftermath, the official court records vanished.

JONATHAN CORWIN, SALEM, 52

His house, a brooding mansion at the crossing of Salem's Essex and North Streets, survives him, one of the last architectural witnesses to New England's largest mass execution. As the residence of the Honorable Jonathan Corwin, it would even play a role in the witchcraft proceedings.

In all ways but one, Corwin's life would emulate his father's. Captain George Corwin inhabited the house most of his life, vacating it as a feeble seventy-five-year-old elder gentleman shortly before his death in 1685. An affluent merchant, he had constructed the gabled home in 1642 after amassing one of the colony's largest estates.

With his death, his son Jonathan occupied the family manse. Like his father, Jonathan served on a hierarchy of courts, starting with small claims, then rising to probate and finally serving on the Superior Court. His career took a detour in 1692, while serving on the governor's ruling council. That year, he would be appointed to a special commission to try witch suspects.

He was a fixture at the hearings, questioning a great number of the accused along with his fellow judge and close friend, Salem magistrate John Hathorne. They would soon be joined by another Salem judge, Bartholomew Gedney. With so many to examine and so few suitable venues, Corwin resorted to using his own home as an impromptu interrogation room. A constable brought the detainee to the eastern front room to stand before him as he questioned her. At other times, he rented a chamber in a local tavern, at public expense. The more formal proceedings involving witnesses and verdicts were held in the Salem meeting-house located at what today is the corner of Essex and Washington Streets.

Corwin had married well. Elizabeth Sheafe, born to a respected Boston family, was the widow of the honored Robert Gibbs, whose father had been knighted by the King. The Gibbs silver plate she had received as a gift from his mother would take pride of place in the Corwin home.

Judge Corwin also held the title to a farm on the southern edge of town, a large if little-used stretch of meadow and woodland with a one-room cabin. He had probably purchased it with the thought of rental income, but with so many more important obligations, it had long stood vacant.

Perhaps it was the farm's location near Salem Town, and its relative neglect, that had brought it to the attention of the Trasks.

William Trask, who owned a Salem fulling mill nearby, had sold the property forty years before. It had passed through at least five subsequent owners before Corwin bought it. Then in 1686, after William's death, his son John laid claim to the property. Though his father had sold it, he had not relinquished his widow's inheritance rights, or so John claimed. Surreptitiously, the Trasks had been harvesting some of its timber. Corwin, no doubt determined to remind them of his position on the court, filed suit.

But if he assumed it would be quickly resolved, he would be mistaken. The litigation dragged on for seven years, testing his patience as he struggled through the most arduous of the witchcraft cases, like a dog constantly nipping at his heels. The case ultimately made its way to the Supreme Court, where it was resolved in 1693.

But in the snows of January, the Trasks got their revenge. As a token of his family's contempt for the witch-hunting absentee landlord, John Trask traveled to the farm with nine men and three ox sleds and stole the cabin, hauling it away board by board. By the time Corwin's hired men arrived, all that was left was a mound of broken chimney bricks.

In March, Corwin would serve Trask with a writ. The miller's son was ordered to appear at the next session of the Essex County Court to answer charges of trespassing and the carrying off of a house and timber. Corwin himself would preside.

With justice thus served and his dignity upheld, he would die a rich and honored man in 1718, more famous than his father and, at seventy-eight, three years older.

BARTHOLOMEW GEDNEY, SALEM, 46

He was a consummate speculator; after suffering significant property losses in Maine, Bartholomew Gedney resolved to be more cautious. Henceforth, he decided to diversify his holdings, though it was all he could do to resist a tempting opportunity.

He had almost lost his shirt. Just before the first Indian war, he purchased thousands of acres in Westcustugo, today's Yarmouth, Maine. A fur trader, Thomas Stevens, sold him the tract, having just bought it from a local Indian chief. Gedney erected a gristmill and two sawmills on the site, but the war broke out and all three were destroyed. At the war's end in 1678, he rebuilt them and, in an added stroke of luck, received a grant for a house plot in nearby Falmouth (now Portland).

Initially, few buyers seemed interested. Then in 1686, after the Spanish forced the English population from Eleuthera Island in the Bahamas, Gedney joined a partnership with the idea of selling them house lots there. In the end, he decided to play it safe, officiating at property closings and executing deeds. Many of the sales were between Massachusetts settlers and the descendents of the tribes who had relinquished them. More than a few interesting documents came his way, providing him with inside knowledge of lucrative deals.

One of them caught his attention in 1687. It was a deed for the purchase of what today is Lynn, Massachusetts, including portions of several surrounding towns. One of the buyers, Adam Hawkes, bequeathed his share to his son and daughter-in-law, John and Sarah Hawkes. Years later, that fortuitous detail would bear fruit.

By 1693, Sarah Hawkes had been widowed. She and her new husband, Samuel Wardwell, were then convicted of witchcraft. He was subsequently hanged. She would survive him, though she would not succeed in winning a reversal of her attainder, which stripped her of all civil rights, including the right to own and bequeath property.

By chance, Gedney would find himself among the trial judges (along with John Hathorne and John Corwin) assigned to handle the property of convicted criminals. The deed to the woman's extensive Lynn holdings was swiftly confiscated, probably to be quietly divided between them.

Gedney may have inherited his entrepreneurial inclinations from his father, the prosperous owner of Salem's Ship Tavern. For years the inn served as the venue for local court sessions. In one ruling reached there, a yoke of oxen was confiscated from a Quaker, John Small, to pay a fine.

Small's wife, still fuming from the fine's injustice weeks later, approached the two magistrates, Daniel Denison and William Hathorne. If her husband and the Friends were such an accursed people, she asked, "how then did they [the magistrates] meddle with their goods? For they must be accursed also." Denison assured her that the goods were given to the poor.

When Gedney's father walked in, the woman turned again to the magistrates. "Is this man the poor you give it to?" she asked. "For it is this man that had my husband's oxen."

"Woman," Hathorne replied testily, "would you have us starve, as we sit about your business?"

Whether Gedney witnessed the exchange is unknown, but in adulthood, he would not go hungry. Along with John Hathorne and Jonathan Corwin, he established himself in Salem as a magistrate. Related by marriage to the Corwins and Winthrops, the trio was virtually inseparable, socializing, praying, and serving together on the Court of Oyer and Terminer. When not ruling on cases, Gedney tended his Salem shipyard, trained the militia, and practiced medicine. All three augmented his earnings.

His wealth and acumen must have imbued him with political clout, as William Stoughton would assign him as one of the three witch court justices required to constitute a quorum. He would be present at many examinations, yet mostly as an observer, letting John Hathorne conduct the interrogations.

One notable exception might have been the May examination of his shipping colleague, John Alden, in Salem Village. Alden, distressed that this longtime acquaintance was not defending him, confronted the magistrate. But Gedney, who had just observed how Alden's mere presence could throw the suffering girls into racking torments, offered no excuses. He had "always look'd upon him to be an honest Man," Gedney replied, "but now he did see cause to alter his judgment."

After his father's death, Gedney would inherit the tavern, now referred to as "Widow Gedney's." Two of his brothers had died. One of their widows, Susanna Gedney, worked in the tavern serving guests. His brother Eleazer's widow, Mary, was tethered to the house, as she had children to tend. But she too procured a liquor license, selling beverages from home. Here again, Gedney's status would prove fruitful, as the witch trial participants were always in need of food and drink.

Later, the General Court received invoices from both of Gedney's sisters-in-law for "entertainment of jurors and witnesses."

JOHN HATHORNE, SALEM, 51

John Hathorne was the third son of nine children born into a family of high ambitions. His father, Major William Hathorne, was a distinguished Salem magistrate and freeholder, having sailed from England on the *Arbella* with John Winthrop. He battled Indians and persecuted Quakers, using land grants to amass what would become an extensive property. When John came of age in 1664, his father gave him his first share of the family estate.

John launched his career keeping books for Salem's merchants, but he soon recognized the rewards of land speculation. By the age of twenty-one, he had become a propertied man and eligible bachelor, yet he wouldn't wed until thirty-three, and then to Ruth Gardner, the fourteen-year-old daughter of a Quaker couple[2] who had fled to Hartford, Connecticut, leaving her in the care of her uncle.

Whether it was the guilt, the taboo, or Ruth's child-like innocence that attracted him is hard to say, but they married in 1675. King Philip's War erupted the same year, but Hathorne prospered. He acquired a wharf and a liquor license, and used the profits to build a mansion in Salem's center, moving in with his youthful bride by the end of the following year. She would bear him five sons and a daughter.

But his success would soon be dimmed by tragedy. Ruth's uncle, Captain William Gardner, was slain fighting Indians that December. Hathorne's younger brother, William, replaced him in the military leadership, then proceeded to gain riches and infamy selling Indian captives into slavery. He died under mysterious circumstances in 1678, leaving a young widow, Sarah Ruck Hathorne.

John's brother Eleazer would lose his life two years later, followed by their father in 1681. Having lost his third brother, Nathaniel, at a young age, John was now the sole male heir. His two surviving sisters married into the Putnam family of Salem Village, leaving John with the vast majority of the Hathorne estate.

His wealth generated opportunity. John Hathorne climbed rapidly up the political hierarchy, becoming a delegate to the General Court and then a member of the governor's ruling Board of Assistants by the age of forty-two. From there he followed his father's footsteps into the judiciary, becoming a justice of the peace and then a judge, traveling throughout Essex County to hear cases. He also kept an eye open for investment opportunities. During a trip to Maine, he bought a nine-thousand-acre tract from a sagamore for a few coins, only to discover that the shifty Indian had sold the same land to several others. The task of tracking each of them down to buy out their titles would prove long and tiresome and preoccupy him for much of his life.

In 1690 he and fellow magistrate Jonathan Corwin were sent on a fact-finding mission to Maine and New Hampshire to look into grievances that Boston was not providing adequate troops to deter Indian aggression. In their report, the two magistrates suggested that the settlers change their tactics. Boston acted on Hathorne and Corwin's recommendations by pulling its troops out. The next day, four hundred to five hundred Indians staged a brutal attack. Houses were burned and settlers killed or captured, sparking months of intense fighting.

Hathorne's next assignment would be closer to home. In 1687 he and two Salem ministers had been asked to mediate a fractious dispute over whether Salem Village should break away from Salem. Instead of recommending that they put the matter to a vote or take other concrete measures, the three recommended that the villagers "act as God shall direct you." They included a prescient warning: Failure to remedy the situation, their report said, would "let in confusion and every evil work."

Five years later, Hathorne would return to Salem Village, this time as chief examiner at the Salem witch trials.

His interrogations were so prejudiced against the accused that the bewitched girls came to rely on his backing. The suspects' guilt was assumed. When Hathorne could not shame them into confessing and naming collaborators, he would trick them, and he had no qualms about intimidating their young children into confessions. He often began examinations by asking the accusing children who was hurting them, and by showing great pity for their condition.

"It is very awful to all to see these agonies," he told Rebecca Nurse, "& you an old Professor [believer] thus charged with contracting with the Devil by the effects of it & yet to see you stand with dry eyes when there are so many whet."

"You do not know my heart," she bravely replied.

Hathorne's haste in convicting the detainees, and his refusal to reconsider a verdict even after major witnesses had recanted their testimony, has left historians wondering if he wasn't profiting materially from his victims' demise. The belongings of convicted witches were routinely seized, ostensibly to pay for their jail expenses. They were also served attainders, which stripped them of their rights, including the right to own or bequeath land. After Samuel Wardwell was executed and his wife sentenced to death, the couple's property in Lynn, Massachusetts, was confiscated and assigned to court officials, including John Hathorne. That case would have personal implications, as Sarah Wardwell had been married to Hathorne's younger brother, William. Even if the judge did not personally benefit from the witchcraft convictions, his calm in the presence of Satan's minions seemed somewhat odd, as he was a devout man who professed belief in satanic power.

Whatever his motives, Hathorne displayed little remorse for sending twenty people to the gallows, nor did his career seem to suffer. In fact, he was promoted. In 1702 he was appointed to the Superior Court. He also retained his seat on Boston's governing Council, leading another fruitless expedition in 1696 against French and Indian forces in Maine before resigning from the bench in 1712. He died in Salem five years later, at seventy-six, and was interred in Salem's Charter Street burial ground. Two of his sons had returned to England; one of them predeceased him, as would his wife, who died at thirty-five in 1695.

A century later, Salem author Nathaniel Hawthorne would apologize for his ancestor's callousness. "I know not whether these ancestors of mine bethought themselves to repent and ask pardon of heaven for their cruelties," he wrote in the introduction to his novel *The Scarlet Letter,* "or whether they are now groaning under the heavy consequences of them, in another state of being."

John Richards, Boston, 48

His was a life of wealth and prestige, but he had earned it the hard way, working his way up from the rank of servant to become one of Boston's wealthiest merchants. By 1692 he was a magistrate, a selectman, the treasurer of Harvard College, and captain of the militia. Major John Richards also happened to be one of the Salem witch trial judges who, like Peter Sergeant and Wait Still Winthrop, remained in the background, doing more listening than talking.

If he did not object to "spectral evidence," which convicted defendants based on the crimes allegedly committed by their apparitions, it was probably due to his strict Puritan beliefs. Richards would have been loathe to spar with his fellow justices, who after all were close friends and business associates.

No one better represented the Boston establishment. He had served for years on the ruling General Court, and had adjudicated numerous court cases. In 1686 he and Samuel Sewall had ruled to suspend Reverend Thomas Cheever, the son of Cotton Mather's former schoolmaster, Ezekiel Cheever, for various improprieties, including using foul language in a Salem tavern.

Richards was one of the longest-standing and most influential members of Boston's North or Second Church, where Increase Mather and his son Cotton co-preached. Cotton felt particularly close to him, with good reason. Of the church's parishioners, Richards contributed the largest sum toward Cotton's salary. He owned property in Mather's neighborhood and lived in a handsome brick mansion. When Cotton married Abigail Phillips in 1686, Richards officiated at the ceremony.

His wealth gave Richards considerable sway not only with the Mathers but with the rest of the congregation as well. Cotton consulted with him on all church affairs of any importance, as he felt Richards would, if necessary, bring the other parishioners around to his views. At times he would be disappointed. Being a staunch conservative, Richards was averse to change and would ignore several of Cotton's proposals.

If anything, the self-made judge seemed to relish his role as the young minister's patron. When the first witch trials began in the spring of 1692, Cotton was too exhausted to attend. Richards urged him to rest at home rather than make the trip to Salem to observe the proceedings. Mather took his advice, writing him a long letter summarizing his views on the witchcraft suspects: that some were incorrigible criminals who deserved to be executed, for example, and that spectral evidence must be taken with a grain of salt.

In September of that year, after three public executions had left the people of Essex County in a state of quiet dread, Richards married Anne Winthrop, the sister of fellow witch trial judge Wait Winthrop. It was his second marriage to a Winthrop. His deceased first wife had been the widow of her uncle, Adam Winthrop. It would be the first marriage for Anne, a spinster, and so welcomed that Lieutenant Governor William Stoughton would officiate.

The ceremony was held at the elegant Boston home of Madame Bridget Hoar Usher, who was in England at the time, and probably included bounteous supplies of cake, wine, beer, and oranges. Among the distinguished guests was Justice Samuel Sewall, who noted it in his diary.

In December of that year, despite sharing responsibility for the execution of twenty innocent people, Richards and five other former witch trial judges were promoted to serve on the newly created Superior Court of Judicature.

His heavenly punishment came two years later. On April 2, 1694, Samuel Sewall wrote in his diary that "In the Afternoon, all the Town is filled with the discourse of Major Richards's Death, which was very extraordinarily suddain." The magistrate had been out on Sunday, "din'd very well" on Monday, then lost his temper with a servant, Richard Frame. Suddenly he passed out in a "Fit of Apoplexy" and never came to. Boston was stunned, as he seemed to be in perfectly good health and was only fifty years old. An autopsy the following evening showed his internal organs to be "fair and sound."

The cause of death was never ascertained. Richards was buried the following day in the family tomb of Boston's North burying point, now known as Copp's Hill Burying Ground. The pallbearers included six of his close friends and fellow magistrates, including Sewall, William Stoughton, Thomas Danforth, and Isaac Addington, while Wait Winthrop escorted his sister, now Richards's widow, to the grave. A Boston foot regiment formed an honor guard. John Richards, one of an illustrious group of Boston magistrates who had drunk toasts at public houses, attended the funerals of each other's children, fought together for the colony's charter, and erred at the Salem witch trials, was now planted beneath the April soil.

NATHANIEL SALTONSTALL, HAVERHILL, 53

The witch trials were intrinsically flawed; Nathaniel Saltonstall sensed it and knew he had to act. Yet try as he might to bring the other judges around, they would not be persuaded, not even his dear friend Samuel Sewall. He could not possibly continue on the bench, so there was nothing to do but resign. He did, yet instead of earning praise, his courageous stance caused him untold grief.

Predictably, some of the finger-pointing girls started seeing his specter. Sewall wrote him a sympathetic note to reassure him that his innocence was beyond question, saying he was grieved "when I heard and saw that you had drunk to excess: so that your head and hand were rendered less useful than at other times."

Weeks later the two crossed paths. Saltonstall was sitting in the Council Chamber at the Boston Town House when Sewall saw him and strode over, inquiring into the health of his father-in-law. Saltonstall told him that Mr. Ward was feeling better, which pleased him. The two talked about the weather, and the fact that the ice was breaking up in the Merrimac River. During a pause in the conversation, Sewall handed him a letter, gesturing that he open and read it. He did so while Sewall waited, observing him. It contained the same message as the last one, more heartfelt pleas that he give up drinking. "Don't furnish your enemies with arms," Sewall had written. Saltonstall thanked his friend and requested his prayers.

Saltonstall had much in common with the other judges, but a wholly different outlook on life. Born into an aristocratic family in Ipswich, Massachusetts, his grandfather, Sir Richard Saltonstall, had sailed from England with Governor John Winthrop and settled Watertown, Massachusetts. He eventually returned to England. Nathaniel's father, Richard Jr., studied at Cambridge University, but returned to Massachusetts, became a magistrate, and won election to the General Court.

Nathaniel was Richard Jr.'s oldest son. He graduated from Harvard in 1659 with nine other students, including the future Boston cleric Samuel Willard. At twenty-four, Nathaniel married Elizabeth Ward. She was eighteen, the daughter of Haverhill's leading citizen, the Reverend John Ward. After their marriage Nathaniel inherited what came to be called Saltonstall Seat, her grandfather's impressive estate.

Five years later, he entered public service, assuming a range of posts from town recorder to clerk of the writs and captain of the militia. He joined the local church, rose to the rank of magistrate, and was elected to represent the town in Boston. He would have stayed on at the General Court, but refused to serve under the despotic royal governor, Sir Edmund Andros.

It was the first test of his political integrity. In 1676 Royal agent Edward Randolph described him as "the most popular and well principled" of Massachusetts's military officers, but as opposition grew to Andros's rule, they branded him a rebel. Eventually they issued a warrant for his arrest.

Saltonstall refrained from adding his name to the list of those demanding Andros's ouster, but after it occurred, he stayed on in his government post. That June he was appointed to the Court of Oyer and Terminer, but quickly grew disillusioned. Distraught by the June 10 execution of Bridget Bishop, he resigned. He had been present at her trial and had serious misgivings about the reliability of spectral evidence. Her death sentence threw him into moral turmoil.

He had always made every effort to protect the innocent. In 1682 he had presided over a Haverhill case involving a local girl, Sarah Davis, who was charged with fornication. Her accuser, Nathaniel Ayer, had fathered her child, though he was married to one of Robert Swan's girls. Saltonstall issued her a fifty-shilling fine, but treated her with respect; he ordered Ayer to pay child support. The decision enraged Ayer's father-in-law, Robert Swan, who complained that Saltonstall had let the girl off easy, while making his son-in-law suffer.

By the autumn of 1692, Saltonstall would learn that the same Sarah Davis had been accused of witchcraft. She had appreciated his kindness—despite the fine— saying he had been like a father to her. Robert Swan's family, on the other hand, was filing witchcraft complaints against all and sundry.

He had listened to his instincts then, and he did so now. "I am not willing," he wrote to the court, "to take part in further proceedings of this nature." His gesture cast aspersions on Governor Phips and Chief Justice William Stoughton and strained his relations with the members of the General Court. When annual elections were held in May of 1693, many of the Oyer and Terminer judges got more votes than they had before the witch trials. Samuel Sewall received the largest count of all. By 1695, the notorious witch prosecutor William Stoughton still ranked among the top three vote-getters, whereas Saltonstall was voted out. Chastened, he withdrew from the public eye.

In 1702 he was appointed to the Inferior Court of Common Pleas for Essex County, a step down from the colony's ruling body, but a respectable position nonetheless.

He served until his death in 1707 from consumption, predeceasing Elizabeth by seven years. By then Judge Saltonstall—who had never been much interested in accumulating real estate—was more propertied than ever. He had inherited his father's eight-hundred-acre Ipswich estate along with a one-hundred-acre farm in Chebacco, a forty-acre Ipswich pasture, and the Haverhill house and property of Elizabeth's father, Reverend Ward.[3]

PETER SERGEANT, BOSTON, 44

Peter Sergeant was already a well-to-do merchant when, at the age of nineteen, he arrived in Boston in 1667. He couldn't have timed it better. He set up shop just as colonial trade was starting to blossom, so he was perfectly positioned to make a fortune. Through a mixture of enterprises and real estate investments, that's exactly what he did.

By 1676 he had staked out some prime real estate and decided to put up the finest mansion in Boston. Before its completion three years later, city records show he was granted permission to build a lime kiln, and in 1680, he was paid for supplying six half barrels of gunpowder used to detonate houses "in the last great fire."

Sergeant's house was palatial indeed—a three-story Jacobean affair made with bricks imported from Holland. Amid the lavish English furnishings was a silk canopy bed in a tapestried chamber. In the back, tiered gardens sloped to a coach house and stable. Two porter's lodges gated the front, from which a paved drive led guests up a long stairway to the porticoed entrance. Crowning it all was an octagonal windowed cupola with a door that opened out onto the gambrel roof and a bronzed weathervane in the shape of an Indian with his bow and arrow drawn. As a final touch, Sergeant had his own initials wrought into the front balcony's ironwork, "16 P.S. 79." Passers-by must have stopped in their tracks, wondering what English nobleman had nested in their midst.

Like most colonial traders, Sergeant's business dealings suffered under the arbitrary rule of Edmund Andros, so in 1689, he actively worked for the governor's expulsion.[4] In the coup's triumphant aftermath, Sergeant was taken into Boston's ruling circles. He headed a committee charged with overseeing public safety in the interim government and, in short order, was admitted to the Third Church. In his diary, Samuel Sewall, a neighbor and fellow church member, mentioned that the deacons arranged to have the church's records and plate stored in a chest in Sergeant's house, it being brick and less apt to burn, as well as highly convenient owing to its location virtually across the street.

Thereafter, Sergeant became an established power broker. At forty-four, he was without question one of Boston's richest men. He helped the colony bankroll the Indian wars, though he was prompt to petition the court when his loans were not repaid. He was appointed to the governing council, then in 1692, when witchcraft became rampant in Salem Village, to the Court of Oyer and Terminer. Yet his name rarely surfaces in the trial records. He remained in the background, perhaps because he lacked legal experience, perhaps because he was busy attending to his commercial activities. There is nothing to suggest that he opposed the court's death sentences or even played a role in doling them out. If anything, the Salem witch trials elevated his standing in the community. By 1700 the church had seated him in the foreseat, the place of honor at the front of the congregation. He remained on the governor's council until 1703, taking a four-year leave of absence, then returning in 1707. Sewall frequently dined with him and two other wealthy witch trial judges, Wait Winthrop and John Richards.

Meanwhile, he had consolidated his wealth through marriage: Each of his four wives came from prosperous merchant families. The first was Elizabeth Corwin, the daughter of Salem shipping magnate George Corwin. After her death, he moved to Elizabeth Shrimpton, daughter of shipowner Henry Shrimpton.

In 1701 Sergeant married the fabulously wealthy Lady Mary Spencer Phips, widow of Governor William Phips. Dame Phips occupied the classy mansion that Phips had built her. After his passing, she gained rights to a wharf, a variety of parcels in Boston's North End, and a large tract on opposite shores of the George River, including islands. Sewall paid the couple a visit shortly after their wedding. They supped, he noted, on "roast beef, venison, pastry, cake, and cheese." Sergeant joined his new wife in the former governor's mansion on the corner of Salem and Charter Streets.

Their union, however, would be brief. Mary Spencer Phips Sergeant died less than five years later and was buried in the Sergeant tomb. "I visit Mr. Sergeant, who takes my visit very kindly," Sewall wrote. He "tells me my Lady would have been 59 years old next March, and that he was two months older." But Sergeant wasted no time finding a replacement. His fourth and last wife, Mehetable Cooper, was a merchant's widow and relative of William Stoughton, the former witch trial judge, who had left Boston property to her.

Yet despite four marriages, Sergeant fathered no children. Perhaps he was too busy acquiring wealth; the records show him filing suit over his second wife's inheritance and transacting various real estate deals. In 1712 he and ten others signed a document granting land for the settlement of Oxford, Massachusetts. The same year he sold a house to a tallow chandler, Josiah Franklin, Benjamin Franklin's father.

Though he shared the bench with the likes of John Hathorne and Samuel Sewall, and undoubtedly was a leading figure in Boston society, Peter Sergeant's name has been consigned to obscurity. If he made any mark at all, it was through his real estate. When the first Earl of Bellomont arrived in 1699 to assume his duties as Massachusetts governor, Sergeant's was the only mansion worthy of him. Approached about the matter, the merchant graciously obliged. He made a few swift repairs, hosted a lavish reception, then humbly moved into a house opposite belonging to William Gibbins. Lord Bellomont died fourteen months later. Ruefully, no doubt, Sergeant returned to his now vacated home.

It came out later that the former witch judge had done rather well by the arrangement. The colony had paid him a handsome rent. For his trouble, it had also reimbursed him for the reception and for what he paid to rent the Gibbins house. What made the deal so sweet was that Sergeant didn't need the money; he had moved in with Mary Phips and sublet the Gibbins house to Charles Hobby.[5]

Samuel Sewall, Boston, 40

Such a huge crowd oared out to gape at a pirate's shipboard execution that the Charles River was covered with boats. Samuel Sewall described the moment in his diary: "When the Scaffold was let sink, there was such a Screech of the Women that my wife heard it sitting in our Entry next the Orchard" at least a mile away.

Months later, Sewall woke from a nightmare: He had been tried and condemned and was waiting to be hanged.

His dream underscores the guilt he must have shouldered throughout his judicial career for sentencing others to their deaths. His diary, fifty years of day-to-day jottings and passing observations, offers a valuable glimpse into the mind of a well-to-do if not always fortunate colonial dignitary. His life was a sloop, rocked to and fro by political currents that he was powerless to change. At times his solution was to put worldly affairs aside and focus on his family. But that could be just as trying. In another of his nightmare scenarios, he dreamed that his wife had perished and that "all my Children were dead except Sarah."

The dream wasn't so far-fetched. Sewall would bury eight of his fourteen children and two of his three wives. In 1678 he almost lost his own life to smallpox, though he had taken earnest measures to avoid it. In addition to dreading the usual house fires, plagues, and natural disasters, he anguished over mundane mishaps, such as the night a thief broke into his house and made off with the silver. As Cotton Mather sat with him one evening and speculated God's purpose in directing lightning strikes onto ministers' homes more often than other peoples', hailstones crashed through the diamond-shaped windows and slid across the floor.

Despite these reversals, his life was relatively happy. Born in Bishopstoke in southern England, Samuel Sewall immigrated to America at the age of nine with his mother and siblings. His father and grandfather had already helped establish Newbury, Massachusetts, in 1635, and it was there that Samuel spent his boyhood, being schooled in Latin, Greek, and Hebrew. He enrolled at Harvard at fifteen, graduating with a master's degree at twenty-two. But his religious ambitions lost out to more worldly interests.

In 1675 Governor Simon Bradstreet would preside at his wedding to eighteen-year-old Hannah Hull, whose father was master of the colony's mint and fabulously wealthy. He would live with her family in an oak-paneled mansion fitted with servants, orchards, a stable, and gardens. His well-connected father-in-law, who lacked sons of his own, would bequeath his sumptuous estate to his new son-in-law, with all its mills, wharves, rental properties, and wilderness tracts.

By the age of twenty-nine, Sewall was the colony's official printer, publishing officially sanctioned books and the sermons of Increase and Cotton Mather. But more prestigious opportunities awaited. In 1683, at thirty-one, he was elected to the General Court, the colony's highest ruling body. Within six months, he had risen to the rank of governor's assistant, and one of New England's most influential figures.

Later oil portraits show a grandfatherly man of comfortable means, conservative but not without warmth, his full figure robed in the black apparel preferred by high officials. An affable sort, he was a familiar face at Boston dinner parties, yet also did his part dousing fires, halting unseemly game playing, and doing night watch. He would amass land and wealth on both sides of the Atlantic, shipping boatloads of whale oil, lumber, beaver skins, and other goods to England and the West Indies, while importing sugar, oranges, cotton, and rum.

When Salem fell under the shadow of witchcraft in 1692, Sewall was one of the magistrates appointed to the Court of Oyer and Terminer. He served from beginning to end, then was reappointed that December to the newly established Superior Court of Judicature.

Yet the witch trials damaged his reputation. In the scandal and recriminations that followed, Sewall underwent a profound change. Three of his children died within four years, in what he surely interpreted as God's punishment for his sins. So in January of 1697, he became the first and only witch trial judge to apologize.

On January 14, 1697, Sewall passed a note to his minister, Samuel Willard, to read before the congregation. It acknowledged his guilt and proclaimed he was ready to atone for his sins. For the rest of his life, he fasted on that date. He also donned a hair shirt of rough, chafing sackcloth each day to remind him of the death and suffering he had caused, and paid calls on the families of those who had suffered from the court's rulings.[6] To add to his grief, he would lose several close family members in subsequent years. Among them were two of his grown daughters, one at age nineteen, the other at thirty-four. Then in 1717, his wife, Hannah, died at fifty-nine. He fared better in his professional life, rising to chief justice of the Superior Court of Judicature. In 1719 he married Abigail Woodmansey Tilley. She would die after seven months, but his third wife, Mary Gibbs, would remain at his side until his death in 1730, at seventy-seven.[7]

Having learned from his mistakes, Samuel Sewall experienced something of a moral awakening that would carry him through his later years. He pressed for an end to the slave trade, whose perpetrators included some of his own friends and kinsmen. His book, *The Selling of Joseph,* would become New England's first abolitionist tract. Sewall also spoke out against the colonists' dismal treatment of Indians, paying the fees so that Indian youths might attend Harvard.

He would spend hours sitting with his invalid daughter, Hannah, who lived on the ground floor of his house, too lame to leave the house. She died in 1724, probably from gangrene, at the age of forty-four. At her deathbed, he composed an essay on the equality of the sexes, expressing certainty that God made no distinction between men and women when they rose into heaven. Hannah would have been proud of him, but she didn't live long enough to read it.

WILLIAM STOUGHTON, DORCHESTER, 61

When Reverend Richard Mather invited him to share his Dorchester pulpit, William Stoughton declined. The twenty-two-year-old scholar would turn Mather down on two more occasions, and when the invitation was renewed fourteen years later, he declined it twice more, at the beginning of the month and again at the end. Six more preaching opportunities came his way, the last in 1670, each of which he rejected.

He had loftier ambitions. Like his high-minded father, he aspired to a life of influence and power, especially in view of his superior intellect. He did not lack for charm, but was frugal with his friendship unless it brought tangible returns. A lean man with a narrow face and long nose, he was a gifted intimidator; people withered under his stare. As chief justice of the Salem witch trial court, he would demonstrate the same inflexibility as he had as a young scholar, brushing caution aside and rushing executions even after the court's methods had been called into serious question.

For William Stoughton, privilege was a birthright. His family left England soon after his birth and sailed to Massachusetts. As the first of Dorchester's settlers, the Stoughtons accumulated a considerable amount of land. In later years, the younger Stoughton would entertain Boston dignitaries at his Dorchester estate, lavishing them with dinners of venison and imported chocolate.

His father, Israel, passed half of his library to the boy at a young age, hoping it would encourage him to cultivate his mind and develop his religious faith. Stoughton did not disappoint. After graduating from Harvard in 1650, he stayed on for a year, then sailed to London to preach. But instead of lining up a church, the young scholar was drawn to Oxford, where he settled in to earn a master of arts degree. He might have continued his studies, but his fellowship was cancelled after the monarchy's restoration in 1660. Seeing little future in a country ruled by Anglicans, Stoughton returned to Dorchester two years later.

Though he had breezed through his divinity studies, he dreaded the idea of becoming an ordained minister. Then in 1671, Stoughton discovered a more attractive alternative: politics. He easily won election to Dorchester's board of selectman, rising to the rank of magistrate three years later. Along the way, he met Joseph Dudley, an aspiring government official who appointed him commissioner for the United Colonies. Thereafter, he held a series of mid-level positions connected to county courts.

By 1676 he was appointed to a committee to answer complaints that Boston was violating the land claims of Mason and Gorges, who were high-placed friends of King Charles II. Other problems needed addressing as well, and Stoughton, being shrewd and articulate, was chosen to hand deliver the colony's reply. He met with several London officials, but they were so distracted by a fictitious assassination plot that Stoughton's party was dismissed. Some in Boston criticized Stoughton for being too compliant, a charge that would be leveled at him some ten years later for his accommodation of the royally imposed governor, Edmund Andros. In his eagerness for political advancement, Stoughton knew when to keep his head down.

For now, Boston rewarded him and the other emissaries with land grants and a whopping hundred and fifty pounds as an expression of "their good affection." When the monarchy cancelled New England's charter and sent Andros to take charge, Stoughton acquiesced. Resistance, he reasoned, might result in an even harsher regime. Twice more he would be appointed as the colony's diplomatic agent, declining both times. He would, however, serve as captain of the Dorchester militia and, in 1680, a major in command of Suffolk County troops.

Though he had inherited his father's property, the Dudley government opened the way to further financial opportunities. In 1682 the two men negotiated a large tract of Nipmuck territory, for which the General Court compensated them a thousand acres each. By now the two were such devoted friends that when Dudley's magistracy was voted down in 1686, Stoughton declined his own election. But Andros would select Dudley as president of the joint colonies and Stoughton as deputy president. His compliance had paid off.

As Dudley's closest friend and adviser, he was soon placed in charge of New England's courts. His backers would excuse his collaboration with the London-installed regime by insisting that Stoughton only took the posts to keep more abusive officials out. But when Andros assumed the governorship in 1686, Stoughton officially became a member of his ruling council. It was a risky move. The colonists considered him a traitor, and even Andros found little to like about the man. Dudley rose to the rank of chief justice the following year, naming Stoughton his assistant. As the political climate darkened, Stoughton retreated into the background. When Andros was evicted in 1689, Stoughton taunted the ousted governor, as if he had despised him all along.

Few were convinced. Like the rest of Andros's government, Stoughton was thrown out and returned to his Dorchester estate to lick his wounds. Cotton Mather meanwhile had been impressed by the erudite man and convinced his father to give him another chance in the government. "Mr. Stoughton is a real friend to New-England, and willing to make any amendment for the miscarriages of the late government," Cotton wrote. "I wish that you might be able to do anything to restore him to the favor of his country."

Increase Mather would indeed bring him back, but no excuses could clear Stoughton's reputation in the public mind. On Mather's recommendation, William Phips appointed him lieutenant governor. Within twenty days of Phips's arrival in Boston, he issued the redeemed official his first task: to sort out the witchcraft problem. Stoughton would do so with zeal. As the chief justice and most aggressive prosecutor at the Court of Oyer and Terminer, he had landed in a prime position to avenge the people of Massachusetts for the indignities they had dealt him during the Andros years.

Convinced that the devil couldn't possibly impersonate an innocent victim, his job was easy: He would condemn every one of the accused suspects. The first, Bridget Bishop, was executed eight days after her trial. By October William Stoughton had presided over the largest mass murder in New England history.

A lifelong bachelor, he exhibited little interest in women and no sympathy at all for their orphaned children. When the trials drew criticism in January of 1693, Stoughton ordered that the last seven convicts be hanged as soon as possible. Advised of the decree, Phips countered it with a reprieve. Stoughton, furious at being overruled, stormed out of the room shouting.

Yet instead of being punished for his zealotry, he would be amply rewarded. Not only was he promoted to chief justice of the newly organized Superior Court of Judicature, but upon Phips's departure for London in 1694, he would rise to the pinnacle of power, acting as the colony's governor for another six years. Thereafter he sat on the ruling council until his death in 1701, at the age of seventy.

He was buried with honor and dignity. Reverend Samuel Willard, who had so fervently opposed Stoughton's ruthlessness during the trials, delivered the funeral sermon. He willed his considerable estate to the town of Dorchester, its church, and to Harvard, a gift so generous that it would take another century to surpass. He would be remembered not as a zealous persecutor, but as a benefactor. In 1726 the town of Stoughton, Massachusetts, was named in his honor.

Wait Still Winthrop, Boston, 50

Conversant in alchemy and herbal remedies, he had all the makings of a wizard. Yet instead of joining the suspects, he adjudicated them at the Salem trials.

Few could match his pedigree. Wait Still Winthrop was a grandson of John Winthrop, founder of the Massachusetts Bay Colony. His father, Connecticut governor John Winthrop Jr., had tinkered with alchemy in his home laboratory. Wait had grown up observing his experiments and perusing his extensive library, which included the colony's largest collection on alchemy, much of it in Latin.

In 1642, the year Wait was born, his father donated forty volumes to Harvard College, but Wait would inherit many more upon his father's death in 1676.

Whether they influenced him or not, Wait practiced medicine when not busy with affairs of state. So effective were his remedies, which he often dispensed for free, that his friend Cotton Mather said of him that "wherever he came the diseased of the place flock'd about him as if the Angel of Bethesda had come among them." Some of his treatments may well have incorporated the hieroglyphic formulas that his father had borrowed from the works of the English magician John Dee. But Increase Mather had mystical texts in his own library. Magic, it seems, was acceptable in the right places.

Named after relatives in the Wait and Still families, he was raised in Connecticut with his older brother, Fitz-John, and four sisters. He took an early interest in political affairs but left Harvard after two years without finishing his degree, fearful of leaving his mother and sisters alone while his father and brother were in England on an extended stay. For the next ten years, he became active in the Connecticut militia. Having inherited property in Massachusetts, he moved to Boston in 1684, just as King James II revoked the colony's charter and installed the widely unpopular royal governor, Sir Edmund Andros.

He and his brother, Fitz-John, served on Andros's council, but couldn't disguise their antipathy to the despot. After Andros's overthrow in 1689, Wait joined the provisional government under Simon Bradstreet and was appointed commander in chief of the militia. When the new charter came into force, he returned to his seat on the governing council in 1692, this time under Governor William Phips. He was a member of Samuel Willard's Third Church and a close friend of such Boston dignitaries as Samuel Sewall and Increase Mather.

With French and Indians attacking the Maine frontier settlements, Winthrop would devote himself to the military as commander in chief of the colony's forces. Now a major general, he would spend months at a time in Maine, requiring his colleagues to hear the witchcraft cases without him.

After the Court of Oyer and Terminer was disbanded, Winthrop was appointed to the Superior Court of Judicature, where he would try the last of the witchcraft cases in 1693. That September, two of his sons died within two days of each other, nine-year-old

William and four-year-old Joseph, of the bloody flux. In the witchcraft episode's final stages, Winthrop seems to have sided with those who felt it had taken a wrong turn, though he never said so publicly. He would resign from the bench in 1701, but seven years later, he became chief justice, a post he would keep for another nine years.

He died in 1717 at seventy-five, having survived his first wife, Mary Browne, and several children. Samuel Sewall, a pallbearer at his military funeral, noted in his diary that the streets "were crowded with people" come to pay their respects. In subsequent years, Sewall would court Winthrop's widow, the fifty-six-year-old Katherine Brattle, but the two never married, as they were unable to reach a prenuptial agreement.

Wait Still Winthrop left a handsome inheritance to his surviving son and daughter, but unlike his famous father and grandfather, he was never revered as a remarkable intellect.

"I am," he told his son in his final words, "verily persuaded that very great and quick changes are coming on the world, and astonishing revolutions, for the overthrowing of things that now seem strongly established."

CHAPTER 5

THE ELITE

In the hierarchy of problems plaguing the Massachusetts leadership in 1692, the plight of Salem's witch suspects ranked near the bottom. More pressing was sheer survival. Confederated Indian tribes were raiding from the north, destroying the tiny settlements that stretched from the interior of Massachusetts to the farthest reaches of the Maine seacoast.

Many communities had been burned to the ground, their inhabitants captured or tortured to death. Traumatized refugees were streaming into Boston. Some chose repatriation in England over the possibility of suffering a violent death at the hands of savages. With the treasury nearly exhausted from the cost of supplying troops, there was little left for the reconstruction of razed villages.

Across the Atlantic, France's empire-hungry Sun King lay in wait, biding his time for an opportunity to choke off England's territorial conquests. The two empires' hostilities were spilling into North America, where the French had found ready recruits in the scattered and disaffected Indian tribes that were being driven or cheated off their tribal lands by English settlers.

In the midst of this instability, the witchcraft crisis broke out in the spring of 1692, adding deeper turmoil to a colony already nearing the political and financial breaking point. Though the hated Governor Andros had been successfully expelled, a new government had yet to succeed him. As Increase Mather negotiated the terms of a charter with the newly coronated King William III and Queen Mary, the home fires were burning perilously low. Simon Bradstreet had stepped in to watch things until his return. But as beloved as the interim governor was, he was eighty-six and feeble. Wary of tackling the colony's dire problems, his Court of Assistants procrastinated, preferring to wait for Mather's return.

SIMON BRADSTREET, SALEM, 87

In the 1630s, while establishing himself in Boston, Simon Bradstreet had prosecuted Quakers and banished heretics, among them Anne Hutchinson. But as his responsibility grew, he lost patience with such things.

There was too much to do. The fledgling colonies were struggling to survive. In 1634 he had forged the New England Confederation, nurturing cooperation and solving disputes between the colonies of Massachusetts, Connecticut, Plymouth, and New Haven for the next thirty-three years. After the English resurrected the monarchy in 1660, he had persuaded King Charles II to grant Massachusetts a modicum of independence, a glimmer of triumph that was followed by gloom. It started with a brutal Indian war that very nearly undid them. Demoralized and broke, they might have succumbed had it not been for their faith in God. After rising to the governorship in 1679, he would spend nine years suturing the wounds.

So in 1680, when a Boston court tried and condemned Newbury goodwife Elizabeth Morse on charges of witchcraft, he let her go. The House of Deputies raised a hue and cry, but he stood firm. Had they forgotten why they had come to this wilderness?

Bradstreet had not. Born in Lincolnshire, he earned his bachelor and master's degrees from Cambridge University. His patron, Thomas Dudley, trained him in the management of wealthy estates, skills he would put to good use under the employ of the Countess of Warwick. In 1628 he married Dudley's sixteen-year-old daughter, Anne, who had barely survived a bout of smallpox. Two years later, they followed her father to the New World, sailing on the *Arbella* in the company of the visionary John Winthrop.

They settled first in Cambridge, Massachusetts. Both he and Dudley were soon elected to government posts, Dudley as deputy governor, Simon as a magistrate serving on the governor's ruling council, then known as the Board of Assistants. Five years later, he and Anne moved up the coastline to Ipswich and by 1645 to Andover, with twenty-two homesteaders.[1]

He built Anne a fine English home near the common, though nothing like the manor houses and sculpted gardens she was used to. The necessary lumber came from his own sawmill on Cochichewick Brook. The mill would do a brisk business, being the only one within miles. Together with his real estate acquisitions and his livestock sales, he and Anne were prospering.

He was away in Boston much of the time on government business. Left alone to raise their eight children, Anne took to penning verse. Centuries later, *she* would be the famous one, not he, despite his honorific titles.[2] Refined and cosmopolitan, they were fish out of water in this frontier settlement of weavers and coopers. Most of their neighbors would be at loose ends in their handsome library, with its eight hundred volumes. He and Anne were in their element.

They would fall to dust in 1666, the same year half of London burned, when a careless servant dropped her candle. Gone were the family oil portraits, the heirloom furniture from Lincolnshire, the carpets and plate, and Anne's precious poems. Soon he would build her a bigger mansion, though by then she showed little interest in earthly possessions. He would learn later that she had much preferred their humbler abode.

In 1670 they would lose their granddaughter Mercy and her baby, having already lost two of her previous infants. Anne never recovered. In 1671 she developed a cough and grew painfully thin. Her arm swelled up with a sore, and a year later, she died, at fifty-nine, with Simon at her side.

They would lay her to rest in the burying ground, where he could glimpse her grave from the window. He grieved for four long years, finally resolving to move on with his life. At seventy-three, he wed another Ann, the widow of Captain Joseph Gardner, who had been slain in Narragansett country during the First Indian War. She was the daughter of Emmanuel Downing, making her a niece of Simon's esteemed friend John Winthrop. Leaving his Andover house in the care of his son Dudley, he moved into her Salem mansion, an elegant three-storied affair right on Main Street.

It was closer to Boston, which proved a good thing, as he was elected governor three years later and would spend much of his time at the Town House in Boston. He served from 1679 to 1686, spending the last two of those years trying in vain to dissuade King James from annulling the colony's charter. He failed, only to be removed from office by a detestable Anglican tyrant. Edmund Andros stepped on every toe, collecting usurious taxes and besmirching their Puritan meetinghouse with Anglican services. The colonists staged a revolution in 1689 and threw him out. Thereafter, to Simon's joy and honor, the people of Massachusetts called him back.

He could not refuse, though he probably should have. At eighty-four, he was not as sharp as he had once been, and the country lay in ruins. With the courts in disarray, the treasury empty, and the war smoldering in Maine, he was not surprised when a group of children fell afoul of witches in 1692. It was the same old foolishness.

To Simon's relief, Reverend Mather reappeared that spring with a new charter. He was less enchanted to learn that an illiterate sea captain would take over the governorship. Phips was too simpleminded to cope with the witchcraft scare, and his deputy, William Stoughton, too ruthless. Spectral evidence was a fraud; it had no basis in Massachusetts law, or even in the Bible. Simon propounded that fact to all who would listen. Unfortunately, few did.[3]

THOMAS BRATTLE, BOSTON, 34

He was born into wealth and blessed with material comfort, plus a good head for numbers. At Harvard Thomas Brattle focused on mathematics rather than theology, which would help him keep the college afloat in later years, when its finances faltered.

In the winter of 1680, as he was finishing his master's degree, the printer John Foster spotted a comet in the sky. Using Harvard's telescope, Brattle and Foster tracked its location. They printed their observations in Boston's 1681 almanac and sent them on to the Royal Observatory in Greenwich, England. From there the notations made their way into Isaac Newton's 1687 masterpiece, *Principia Mathematica*. It was a great honor.

Brattle then traveled to England, making business contacts and being inducted into London's elite Royal Society. His father, who had founded Harvard with John Hull of Boston's Third Church, left him a generous inheritance.

Upon his return, he plunged into trade, marking each purchase and expense in his account books in a tight and legible hand. As his profits swelled, so did his pleasures. His home was opulently furnished, all the better to entertain his ever-widening circle of Boston acquaintances, most of them Puritans or Harvard classmates.

But the harshness of Puritan worship didn't sit well with the liberal-minded Thomas Brattle. He felt more at home with the Church of England, a rival denomination whose ritual and gilded ostentation were anathema to the Puritan elite and prohibited by law until the new charter reversed the ban. There hadn't been a single Anglican church in New England until Sir Edmund Andros opened King's Chapel in Boston in 1686. Brattle remedied that problem in 1699. For now, he openly admitted his Anglican leanings, though opponents called him an "apostate" and "infidel."

A man of his wealth could afford to embrace unpopular causes. As a Harvard tutor, he had dared suggest that his students might wish to read Anglican as well as Puritan texts. Instinctively critical of Puritan teachings, he paid all the more attention to the events of 1692, when the stridently Puritan Salem Village was overwhelmed by witchcraft. The judges seemed overly hasty, as if acting on foregone conclusions, and the testimony spurious, especially spectral evidence. By October of that year, Brattle had started distributing a manuscript-length "letter,"[4] adding himself to a list of prominent Bostonians who "do utterly condemn" the trials. Among others, the list included former governor Simon Bradstreet, former deputy governor Thomas Danforth, the Boston ministers Increase Mather and Samuel Willard, and Justice Nathaniel Saltonstall.

Public opinion was already turning against the proceedings, especially after the fourth and final mass execution on September 22. Brattle joined the disparaging chorus. His resistance became so impassioned that he allied himself with his nemesis, the ultra-Puritan Reverend Increase Mather. In October the two visited Salem jail, where several detainees admitted that they had lied. In his missive, Brattle would describe the "rude and barbarous methods" that had been used to obtain their confessions and how mercilessly some of the husbands had treated their slandered wives. He was particularly appalled at the situation in Andover, which suffered more accusations than any other community. "They lament their folly," he wrote of the town, "and are an object of great pity and commiseration."

At the peak of his efforts, Brattle swapped his pen for his purse. As the Andover debacle was dying down, the afflicted group accused "a worthy gentleman of Boston." The individual, who was never named, responded swiftly, threatening the accusers with a thousand-pound defamation suit. That seemed to quell the Andover witch hunt. Whether Brattle was the gentleman in question is not clear. But considering his wealth and Anglican leanings, it is likely that he would have been targeted, as was Salem merchant Phillip English, another wealthy Anglican.

In the aftermath of the crisis, Harvard president Increase Mather appointed Brattle as the college's treasurer after John Richards's death. He probably regretted it, as Brattle had quietly been working toward the establishment of the Anglican Brattle Street Church, which opened in 1699. "A moral heathen would not have done as he has done," Mather groused about the plan.

He complained less about the merchant's financial acumen. Brattle would deftly expand the school's financial assets until his death in 1713, in part by relentlessly dunning debtors.

He applied the same financial discipline in his will. Being a lifelong bachelor, he had no heirs and so bequeathed most of his fortune to public institutions. Two hundred pounds went to Harvard. He asked that a ring be bestowed on each of Harvard's fellows, on its president, and on Benjamin Coleman, the minister of the Brattle Street Anglican Church. He also left it his organ, asking that within a year of his death, the congregation procure "a Sober person that can play skillfully thereon with a loud noise."[5]

Most ingeniously, he instructed the executor of his will to issue bills of credit in the same quantity as his age at the time of his death, to be distributed among the poor. The bills were to be handed out by his three sisters. An equal number were to be given to the colony's neediest ministers.

As a postscript, Brattle requested that half a crown be given to every Harvard student who showed up for his funeral.

ROBERT CALEF, BOSTON, 44

A prosperous textile merchant, Robert Calef became so incensed over the mishandling of the Salem witchcraft trials, and over Reverend Cotton Mather's role in provoking them, that the preacher sued him for slander.

Described variously as a weaver, clothier, and textile shop owner, Calef was much more than that. He owned shares in four vessels, one of which was captured by the French in 1696. He served in Boston as constable for a time in 1692, which may have compelled him to take a closer look at the Salem proceedings.

Even before the witch crisis got out of hand, Calef's liberal views predisposed him against Massachusetts's conservative leadership, especially the two Mathers. Family lore suggests that this university-educated importer probably left the old country because he opposed England's persecution of the Quakers.[6]

Once in Massachusetts, he married Maria Trace. They had nine children, most if not all of whom survived into adulthood. In Boston he opened a cloth-making business and joined the First Church. By 1690 he was managing three estates, and in 1691 he was appointed constable. Since few of the witchcraft suspects were living in Boston, Calef would have arrested few, if any. But early in 1693, after the trials were largely over, seventeen-year-old Margaret Rule was overcome with seizure-like symptoms that closely resembled demonic possession.

Reverend Cotton Mather took the young woman into his home, as he had done with other afflicted children, and encouraged the community to show their support. Dozens of fascinated spectators mobbed her room. When Calef entered with a few friends, the girl was shrieking and gasping for breath but soon became jolly and talkative. She primped, flirted with an old boyfriend, and groused that some people thought she was faking. Calef consulted with her attendants and tried to ascertain what was causing her stiffness and convulsions, but Margaret's friends shooed him out. He quickly concluded that she was suffering from nothing more than a case of nerves. He confronted Mather with his suspicions, but their conversation became so heated that the preacher insulted him and stomped out of the room.

What followed was a long and vitriolic battle of words. Fearing a new wave of accusations, and perhaps regretful that he hadn't done more to avert the first one, Calef decided to act. "I thought it my duty," he would write, "to be no longer an idle spectator."

In September of 1693, he wrote up and circulated an injurious account of his two visits to Margaret Rule, asserting that the girl was only pretending to be ill and that Cotton Mather had tried to revive her by feeding her rum and fondling her breasts and stomach. To the Mathers' despair, the report became the talk of the town. Whether it was true or not is open to question, but as Mather would remark later, had he wanted to molest the girl, he wouldn't have done it in front of forty witnesses.

A week later, Mather filed a lawsuit against Calef for his "pernicious libels." He would also vent his anger from the pulpit. In reply, Calef suggested they settle their differences in person at John Wilkins's book-store. Mather agreed, but never appeared, as his small daughter, Mary, started vomiting worms and had to be taken out of Boston.

Over the next four years, Calef sent a series of scathing letters to the junior Mather, demanding explanations for his theories and ridiculing the cleric's vague replies. Mather dropped the suit but continued a sporadic reply to his letters, suggesting condescendingly that Calef come and work in his library to educate himself.

In August of 1697, Calef finished a strident manuscript denouncing the trials, with emphasis on their flaws and incompetence. He referred to the afflicted girls as "vile varlets" and "lying wenches" who had accused their innocent neighbors, encouraged by bloodthirsty magistrates and ministers who had lured them on with "bigoted zeal." He titled it *More Wonders of the Invisible World* in mockery of Cotton Mather, who had previously published a history of the witch trials with the name *Wonders of the Invisible World.*

By now his relations with the Mathers were so hostile that no Boston printer would publish the book. A London publisher finally did, though it wouldn't make its way to Boston until 1700. In his role as president of Harvard, Increase Mather ordered "the wicked book" burned in the college yard. Calef had sent copies to both of the Mathers, with a copy to the governor. In self-defense, the Mathers issued a retort with the long-winded title *Some few remarks on a Scandalous Book against the Government and Ministry of New England, by one Robert Calef, detecting the unparalleled malice and falsehood of said book, composed and published by several persons belonging to the flock of some of the injured pastors, and concerned for their justification.*

Calef's determination to prosecute the unrepentant Cotton Mather seems not to have hurt him financially. In December of 1695, he and fellow shopkeeper Thomas Bannister paid a two-hundred-pound bond to keep Quaker shopkeeper Thomas Maule out of jail. Maule had been arrested for publishing yet another denunciation of the witch trials, which was confiscated and burned.

Despite his outspoken views, Calef held several civic posts, among them appraiser, fence viewer, and clerk of the market. He consulted at inquests, arbitrated disputes, and acted as overseer of the poor. Judge Samuel Sewall paid visits to discuss Boston charities.

In 1710, at the age of sixty-two, Calef and his wife moved to Roxbury, where he served as selectman. He also set up a weaving operation and dye house, bought and leased land, and dabbled in foreign trade. It was there that they would lose their youngest child, Daniel.

Calef himself died in 1719, at seventy-one. In his will, he left the entirety of his holdings to his wife. It was an unusual gesture, as the common practice was to leave one's widow some livestock and part of the house to live in. Land and buildings were traditionally left to sons. But Calef's gesture was consistent with his principles, and the mutual respect he and his wife shared. Maria Trace Calef, his companion for fifty years, followed her husband to the grave seven months later.

THOMAS DANFORTH, CAMBRIDGE, 70

As the oldest son of six children, Thomas Danforth grew accustomed to family responsibilities from an early age. His mother died young. His father, Nicholas Danforth, increasingly relied on his son for help raising his younger siblings. In 1634, when Thomas was twelve, the motherless family would leave their home in Framlingham, England, and make the ocean voyage to New England.

The religious practices there were more to his father's liking. At home, they faced constant harassment for refusing to attend the Anglican church. They settled in Massachusetts, but within four years, his father would die, leaving Thomas to head the family, though he was just fifteen.

He would rise to the challenge. Years later, he would raise his own children, this time with the help of a wife. In 1644 he married Mary Withington, who bore him twelve children, six of whom would die before the age of two. Indeed, only two of Thomas Danforth's children would still be alive at the time of his death, both of them daughters.[7]

But Danforth did not allow his private sorrows to interfere with his public obligations. A year after his marriage, he put his name on the ballot for Cambridge's selectman and town clerk, and was elected. It would mark the beginning of a fifty-year career that, despite lacking a formal education, would land him near the pinnacle of the Massachusetts leadership. As stepping-stones, he served as treasurer of Middlesex

County, treasurer and then steward of Harvard College, and judge of the Superior Court. As a magistrate,
he made his way into Boston's highest ruling circles.

At the peak of his power, he would serve as deputy
governor under Simon Bradstreet, a mild-mannered
and diplomatic leader whom he would probably have
succeeded had Bradstreet not continued to serve into
his eighties. Like other magistrates, Danforth tended
to various businesses on the side. He inherited property from his father, which he supplemented with
additional purchases, including hundreds of acres
along the Sudbury River, a site he named Framingham
after his English birthplace.

Leading a contingent of sixty armed men, he traveled to Casco Bay in 1680, setting himself up in York
and doling out land parcels to settlers. He also created
the area's first governing council, placing himself at
its head. At the time, Maine had yet to merge with the
Massachusetts Bay.

Over the next nine years, he would settle land
claims, negotiate Indian treaties, and lay out street
plans for Falmouth, in what is now Portland. His
brother Jonathan, a Billerica surveyor, may have
assisted. A second brother, Samuel, was preaching in
Roxbury with the Indian teacher John Eliot.

Danforth was a close friend and neighbor of Cambridge magistrate Daniel Gookin, who acted as Super-
intendent of Indians. He would support Gookin and
Eliot in their efforts to convert Massachusetts tribes to
Christianity and organize them into anglicized "praying towns." In the midst of the Indian wars, when the

converts were harassed by English settlers, Danforth came to their defense, even though he had lost a son in the battle against Rhode Island's Narragansetts. He and Gookin received death threats for their defense of Indian allies; in the aftermath of King Philip's War, both raised Indian orphans.

During the ill-fated Andros regime, Danforth resisted the Crown's attempts to subjugate Massachusetts, issuing veiled threats that the colony might rise up in revolt. After Andros's removal, he was serving in Simon Bradstreet's interim government when Massachusetts constables started rounding up witch suspects. When they arrested Salem tavern owner John Proctor, Danforth decided to look into the situation and rode to Salem to conduct the examination.

He had been wary of witchcraft cases ever since he dealt with one in 1659. A young mother had accused an elderly widow and her adult daughter of causing them harm. Acting as Cambridge magistrate, Danforth had arrested the two women, but failing to see what danger they could pose, he released them. The women then filed a defamation suit, though the jury dismissed it, arguing that the young woman, Rebecca Stearns, had not been in her right mind when she hurled the accusation. It had all boiled down to nerves. He had jailed another witch suspect, Chelmsford goodwife Martha Sparks, as recently as 1691, but made no efforts to try her. So when the new governor arrived amid the 1692 witchcraft trouble, Danforth was pleased to withdraw.

The seasoned Bradstreet was replaced by the untried Phips. More ominously, Danforth would relinquish his office to William Stoughton, a relentless prosecutor who had predetermined the suspects' guilt. Thereafter, Danforth worked behind the scenes.

Having served almost twenty years alongside Boston's elite, he had a wide circle of acquaintances. Though it is uncertain where he started, Samuel Sewall later noted how much Danforth did "to end the troubles under which the country groaned in 1692."

Since he leaned away from ostentation, whether it be the painting of a portrait or simply keeping a diary, his efforts are all that much harder to discern. Many official reports are attributed to his hand, even though they were credited as the work of Governor Bradstreet or Increase Mather. In 1699, at the age of seventy-seven, Danforth's under-acclaimed career would end, as would his life.[8]

Philip English, Boston, 41

He heard footsteps on the stairs, then a knock at his bed chamber—a servant, no doubt, notifying him of a late-night visitor with urgent business. He was mistaken; it was the sheriff, with a warrant for his arrest.

As Salem's wealthiest merchant, Philip English may have assumed no one noticed his French accent. A native of Jersey, an isle off the coast of Normandy, he had come to Massachusetts as a child, anglicized his name, and married into a merchant family, the Hollingworths. Yet no one was fooled. France was England's sworn enemy, using Indians as its pawns in a war of attrition aimed at driving the English from Massachusetts.

Even an international merchant of his prominence—with a sumptuous gabled mansion, a wharf, and over twenty merchant vessels—was not immune in 1692, when the people of Massachusetts were classed into one of two groups: the godly sort and Satan's minions. If anything, English's mercantile success made him a bigger target.

It was people like these, the reasoning went, who were responsible for the colony's moral backsliding. Profits were overtaking principles. English, making use of his French background, had outdone his competitors, cultivating markets in such little-known ports as Spain, France, and Portugal, rather than the usual England and West Indies. It was people like English who had brought so many to financial ruin on the Maine frontier, where land investments once deemed wise were now proving disastrous.

Speculators had bargained with godless natives and incited them to war. Now the "heathens" were killing, bringing their war whoops closer to Boston, slaying the soldiers sent to protect the merchants' commercial holdings, while the traders themselves were enjoying lives of comfort.

Salem's indigent farmers must have ogled the family's estate. It was a world of servants, orchards, and landscaped gardens. They hosted lavish dinners and sent their two daughters to a posh finishing school. Mistress English surrounded herself with luxuries, running a shop from the side of their mansion selling everything from ribbons to ready-made shoes.

Now, perhaps, they would regret their Sunday pilgrimages. Every Sabbath, the Englishes sailed to Marblehead to St. Michael's Anglican Church. That alone must have antagonized this Puritan community, and foolishly, they had made a show of it, singing and laughing as the vessel drifted off.

In March of 1692, only weeks before his arrest, English had taken office as a town selectman. Perhaps that had instigated it. His presence reflected the shift from a rural community to a more commercial one.

Thinking quickly, English welcomed the sheriff. He listened while the arrest warrant was read, then asked if the sheriff might return for them the following morning. His wife was not presentable. Once the sheriff had left, they made their escape.

They would be rearrested, jailed this time in Boston. Philip English posted enough bond—four thousand pounds sterling—to place his family in the jail keeper's house, away from the stench and rabble of common prisoners. They were free to leave during the day as long as they returned at night. Their friends mobilized, and two sympathetic clergymen, Reverends Willard and Moody, helped hatch a second escape. This one would work. The couple left their daughters in the care of trusted friends, then made haste to New York, where they would wait the crisis out.

When they emerged from hiding in the spring of 1693, the Englishes found their house looted and wrecked. Salem Sheriff George Corwin had gone in with his men and seized everything moveable, at least a thousand pounds worth. Clapboards were ripped off the house. Personal items, such as family portraits and items of clothing, were stolen. The larder was emptied of wines and provisions, and the warehouses cleaned of cod, grain, fish hooks, and lumber. The livestock was missing, including six pigs and "a certain cow with a bob tail." Even Mary's little shop had been robbed of its goods, down to the three gross of thimbles. English drew up an inventory of his losses and filed a suit, but the litigation lasted decades. He would never recover it all. The settlement he did receive fell far short of his demands, so as a parting gesture, Philip English bestowed a gift.

In 1734, when Puritan laws had loosened enough to allow it, he donated land toward the construction of St. Peter's, Salem's first Anglican church.

SIR WILLIAM PHIPS, BOSTON, 41

Had he not replaced Simon Bradstreet as governor, the Salem witch hunt might have been averted. But the colony's leadership was for London to decide. And for the English monarchy, William Phips had appeal. He was everything Bradstreet was not: brawny, secular, pliable, and beholden to the Crown.

Phips was born in 1651, the youngest of the six children of a blacksmith and fur trader in Woolwich, in the outermost Maine frontier.[9] As a youth, he farmed and herded sheep until the age of eighteen, when he spent four years as a shipbuilder's apprentice.

What he lacked in education, William Phips made up for in personal magnetism. He had a masculine charm and likeability that won people over, despite occasional flare-ups and foul language. While working as a shipwright in Boston, he was schooled in basic literacy, but it is doubtful that he was ever able to write more than his own name. As governor, when he complained that a letter had been written in Dutch, an aide insisted it was English.

At the age of twenty-two, Phips married Mary Spencer Hull, the widow of Boston's fabulously wealthy goldsmith, merchant, and mintmaker, John Hull. Phips had been on the lookout for moneymaking opportunities, and now he had the use of her vast capital to build a shipyard on his father's Kennebec River property. But Indian tribes were joining forces to push back the land-grabbing English, and the site came under attack. By luck, one of the newly built ships was ready to launch. Phips jumped aboard with his family and crew and escaped, abandoning the cargo. The shipyard was burned to the ground, and a merchant, Thomas Lake, was killed. Though everyone else survived, Phips's creditors would sue him for unpaid loans and his failure to deliver the lost cargo. Phips found himself under such financial pressure that when handed an eighty-five-pound invoice, he fell into a rage and threw it in the fire.

Tales were going around about Spanish gold in a shipwreck near the Bahamas. Phips was in his element at sea and could handle tough sailors. Since treasure seemed the fastest path to wealth, he captained a few expeditions. They must have been profitable, as six of his crewmen sued him for withholding their shares of the take. After various other small finds, Phips decided to go for something big. The Spanish galleon *Concepcion* had gone down in 1641 on a coral reef about eighty miles north of Hispaniola, now Haiti and the Dominican Republic. Phips had a hunch about it. Back in England, he had relatives with high connections and decided to enlist their help in the recruitment of wealthy patrons. His cousin, Sir Constantine Phipps, was the Lord Chancellor of Ireland.

Though lacking the refinement and credentials required in such circles, he managed to win financial backing not only from private patrons but also from King Charles II himself. The monarch loaned him a warship, the *Rose,* equipped with guns, supplies, and two royal observers.

The first expedition failed. His heavy-drinking crew, who were paid in shares of discovered treasure, raped and pillaged at various ports of call. Near Boston, two of them assaulted one of the king's onboard agents, who disembarked in a huff and returned to London on another vessel. Phips then fell afoul of Boston authorities by firing at vessels in Boston harbor that failed to acknowledge the *Rose*'s royal status, then demanding that they reimburse him for the wasted ammunition. The complaints became so heated that Governor Bradstreet personally went down to tell Phips off.

Back at sea, he would have to quell two attempted mutinies. In his romanticized biography of the future governor, Reverend Cotton Mather would describe him facing the would-be pirates with their swords drawn, "though he had not so much of a weapon as an ox goad or a jaw bone," taking them down with his bare hands.

Yet he returned to London virtually empty-handed, an embarrassment made only slightly more bearable by the fact that Charles II had died. Two years later, King James II would give him a second chance. This time Phips struck pay dirt, raising a three-hundred-thousand-pound fortune in Spanish gold and silver. Once the king and patrons were paid off, Phips got eleven thousand pounds, a vast amount for the time. A London celebrity, he was knighted at Windsor Castle and appointed to the impressive post of provost marshal under Boston's newly imposed royal governor, Edmund Andros. Sir William Phips returned to Boston in triumph, a lowly laborer turned gentleman of means.

He trumpeted his new prestige by building a handsome brick mansion on Green Lane, today's Charter Street. He probably rejoiced to see Simon Bradstreet, who had scolded him years before, ousted from office, but Andros proved anything but cordial. Since Phips was barely literate and woefully unprepared for his elevated post, his days would be numbered. But before sailing to London to resign, he heard Cotton Mather preach at the North Church. The two men bonded, and Phips agreed that while in London he would help Cotton's father, Increase Mather, in his campaign to win back the colony's charter.

When he next returned, he would find Boston in euphoric celebration. The colonists had overthrown the detested Andros and replaced him with their respected former governor, Simon Bradstreet. This time Phips sided with the colony. Now a member in good standing of the Mathers' North Church, he was a close confident of both prominent reverends, father and son, who helped him in being assigned to crucial military expeditions. The first was the May 1690 effort to seize Port Royal from the French. Being near Maine, his old stomping grounds, this was relatively successful. But his siege of Quebec two months later would end in disaster. In the interim, Increase Mather had persuaded the monarchy to restore the colony's charter, using his influence to get Phips appointed as royal governor. Though Mather was patently aware of Phips's shortcomings, at least Mather would retain some influence over the colony's leadership.

In May of 1692, the two returned to a colony gripped with fear. The jails were overflowing with witch suspects awaiting trial, and new suspects were being unmasked faster than the constables could bring them in. Flustered, the new governor turned to his advisory council for advice. Some of its members had been interrogating suspects in his absence. Since the colony still lacked courts, and perhaps to address the gravity of the situation, Phips appointed an ad hoc tribunal to try the suspects, the Court of Oyer and Terminer. To head it, he appointed the most uncompromising of the group, Deputy Governor William Stoughton. Phips also ordered that the suspects be locked in irons, as their spirits were running rampant, torturing helpless children.

Then he withdrew, feeling more comfortable tending the Indian threats in Maine. Rebecca Nurse's family, desperate to save her from execution, petitioned him for a reprieve. He consented, until "some Salem Gentlemen," probably John Hathorne and John Corwin, changed his mind. John Proctor's petition got no reply at all. Nor did he give London any inkling of the crisis under way, at least not yet. What seems likely is that Phips supported the trials until public opinion turned against them.

In August he traveled to war-torn Maine to check on defenses, returning to find the trial situation in disarray. Increase Mather was having grave doubts, especially about using apparitions, or specters, to prove a suspect's guilt. Phips also worried that "the Devill had taken upon him the name and shape of several persons who were doubtless innocent." Having no shortage of enemies, he may have feared his own arrest. He was known to have consulted fortune-tellers and had myriad connections to Maine. One of Lady Phips's relatives had been accused of witchcraft in the 1650s. During his absence, she had willfully signed an order demanding the release of a witch suspect. The jailer had hesitantly complied, and now some were implying that even she might be a witch.

The executions had gotten out of hand, and bickering had broken out at the highest levels of government. In desperation, Phips wrote to London. He broke his silence about the crisis, downplayed the extent of the chaos, and defended himself against the magistrates' excesses, saying he had been preoccupied with the war. He would await London's orders before taking further steps. For safety's sake, he put a stop to the hangings and chastened Stoughton for his relentless convictions. Later Phips would abolish the Court of Oyer and Terminer and set up a proper court system.

"Next to divine providence," he would write, "it is the stop to these proceedings which has averted the ruin of this province."

His actions ended the debacle, but his reputation would never recover. The criticism wouldn't stop, not only for his ineptitude during the witch hunt but also for failing to stem the bloodletting on the Maine frontier. Eager to acquire land while he still could, he arranged the purchase of Waldo County from the Maine Indian chief, Madockawando.

Less than a year after signing the deed, before he could legitimize his claim, he was summoned to London to answer charges of embezzlement. Arrested upon arrival, he took sick there in 1695. His fever turned into influenza, and at forty-four, he died.[10] Four years later, the now widowed Lady Phips would marry Peter Sergeant, one of the magistrates whose rulings hastened William Phips's demise.

Britain's King William III and Queen Mary

They made an odd-looking pair. She was exceptionally tall and handsome, while he was short and asthmatic. But then, personal wishes never counted for much in the political chess game of royal marriages. Mary Stuart knew that. Even so, she broke into tears when she learned that she was to marry her cousin William of Orange, Stadtholder of the Netherlands. She wept during the wedding and continued weeping as the coach whisked them to Holland.

She had inherited dueling faiths. Though the daughter of King James II, who had converted to Catholicism, she was raised as a Protestant. At her birth in 1662, the English monarchy was still adapting to its recent restoration. Only two years before, Oliver Cromwell's Puritan experiment had collapsed. But her father had proved a dismal ruler, and then at fifteen, she had wed William in an arranged marriage.

They would live in Holland until opposition to her father's Catholic policies had grown so heated that a group of English nobles had decided to overthrow him. William and Mary were offered the throne, an invitation they graciously accepted. Armed with Dutch troops, William invaded England in 1688, forcing Mary's father into French exile. His voluntary departure was a gift, as it spared the family the turmoil of capturing or beheading him. There would be long-anticipated improvements under William and Mary, including a bill of rights limiting royal power and giving Parliament control over the treasury and the army.

Though queen by name, Mary would assume a mostly ceremonial role, her days dissolving into a blur of banquets and ladies-in-waiting. In Holland she had taken a liking to Delft designs, which now found their way into English porcelain, gardening, and decor. William occupied himself with affairs of state, be it battling the hostile French, dispelling Popish plots, quelling Scottish intransigence, or easing the travails of the distant colonies.

Ruled by Puritan fanatics, New England was by turns deferential and intractable. The colonists bristled at any constraints on their own faith, yet refused to tolerate any other, particularly Quakers or Anglicans. They also violated London's Navigation Acts and snubbed their noses at royal land claims, all of which had forced Mary's grandfather, Charles II, to abolish their charter and send a royal emissary, Sir Edmund Andros, to take control.

Andros's 1689 eviction was triggered by William's own invasion; at least both were bloodless. A distinguished New England cleric, Increase Mather, had spent four years in London trying to persuade James II to allow Massachusetts a degree of self-rule. With the monarch's sudden flight into exile, Mather had to start all over with William and Mary. So far, the negotiations had been fairly congenial.

He was an impressive gentleman, sober and learned, with reasonable requests. They were surprised at how comfortable they felt with this devout Puritan, as if chatting with a Londoner rather than a wilderness preacher, and indeed, Reverend Mather seemed in no great hurry to sail back. In sharp contrast, his associate, Sir William

Phips, was more of what you'd expect of a New England frontiersman, vulgar and ill-mannered.

At last, the king consented to Mather's suggestion that Phips be governor. A treasure hunter and some-time pirate seemed an odd choice for the colony's top position, but Mather spoke highly of his military skills. That being the most important, William relented, but only on the condition that henceforth, the Crown would be the one to select the colony's governor. Mather had heartily concurred. William offered no objections at all to Mather's magisterial candidates, and soon after, William III, King of England, Scotland, and Ireland, put his signature and seal to the new Massachusetts charter and extended his hand for Mather and Phips to kiss.

It was October of 1691. The two set out right away on the return journey, but it would be months before they dropped anchor in Boston harbor. They clearly survived the dismal voyage, as the next thing William knew, missives were piling up from Governor Phips. Most were about the Indian wars, and how badly they were going. His vaunted military skills hadn't been so impressive after all. But one of the dispatches mentioned something new: that a village near Boston was inundated with witches. The letter ended with a request for royal guidance.

In reply, William ordered the construction of a new fort in Maine, thinking it might stem French and Indian incursions and demonstrate England's resolve. As for witches, Phips would have to use his own judg-ment. Whitehall had more important things to worry about. The King had sent troops to the Spanish Neth-erlands (now Belgium) in a conflict that was bogging down. Partisan infighting in Parliament was handicapping his foreign policies, and he was battling to preserve what few royal prerogatives he had left. To make matters worse, Mary's sister, Anne, was plotting against them with her wily courtiers John and Sarah Churchill.

When William found time to turn his attention to his far-flung colonies, he was not pleased at what he learned. Phips had been so preoccupied with his wretched witches that he had botched the war effort, leading a disastrous campaign against the French and Indians in Quebec. William had ignored the many complaints that the man was a cowardly fool who deserved hanging, thinking he'd give the lad the time to prove himself. But now there were whispers of embezzlement, and at that, he drew the line. Phips, it seems, had been pocketing the King's tenth, the percentage owed the Crown of any booty captured by privateers. Rather than arrest Phips outright, William opted to call him home and let him answer to the charges in person. The summons, signed in February of 1694, didn't arrive in Boston until that July.

He couldn't help but sympathize with Mary's frustration at how slowly messages were delivered. A year earlier, she had sent a letter ordering that Boston establish a proper postal system. The missive, after ten months in transit, was read to Phips, but ignored.

In December of that year, Mary, Queen of England, Scotland, and Ireland, would die childless at thirty-two. Though initially estranged, the couple had grown inseparable. The news of her death, and the curious fact that it came after a mere four-day struggle with smallpox, reached Boston fifteen months later.

CONCLUSION

Did Seventeenth-Century Living Conditions Predispose English Settlers to Witch Hunts?

The Court of Oyer & Terminer adjourned for the last time on September 22, 1692. The executions were over, though the witch trials would drag on under a different court until 1693. Even if the judges had yet to see the error of their ways, the colonists had had enough. By the end of that summer, several prominent individuals had openly condemned the notion of issuing death sentences on the basis of spectral evidence.

The most strident critics, whose wealth and prestige lent them a certain immunity, stood at the crest of this critical wave. Thomas Brattle, Harvard's treasurer, was probably the loudest, followed by Boston entrepreneur Robert Calef. Members of Simon Bradstreet's interim government, still esteemed even if no longer in power, stood behind them.

The clergy, though also alarmed at the court's excesses, was not as bold. Increase Mather essentially conducted his own independent investigation before taking a stand, interviewing accusers and victims. Since a fellow clergyman, Reverend George Burroughs, had been convicted and hanged, all but the most powerful clerics treaded with caution. Reverend Samuel Willard spoke out after one of the afflicted girls accused him in court. By contrast, Andover's Francis Dane mobilized his entire community in a frantic campaign to rescue the village's jailed women and save his own family— two of whom had already been hanged.

Of the judges, only Nathaniel Saltonstall had the integrity—and the backbone—to break ranks with his fellow magistrates and, when they would not listen, resign from the court. Samuel Sewall harbored doubts, but dared not act on them until it was too late. At least he would admit his guilt and ask forgiveness. The others went on with their privileged lives, unrepentant and unpunished. The worst of them, William Stoughton, even rose to the pinnacle of power, standing in for two royal governors who died in office, William Phips and Richard Coote. Rather than condemning Stoughton, the Massachusetts leadership immortalized him, naming a town and a Harvard dormitory in his honor.

Today we can only wonder how such seasoned judges could have believed the frenzied slurs of the "afflicted" children. Perhaps, as historians have suggested, they willfully ignored the obvious truth because it seemed like one disturbance they could control. Their efforts to quell the Indian bloodletting in Maine had met with utter failure. Perhaps they quickly realized their mistake, but were loathe to admit it and endure public censure.

But a more important question might be this: What provoked the "bewitchings" in the first place? What caused these young people to fall into hysterical fits? An answer might be found in their private lives. Most were preteens, though some were young adults, and a few were in their thirties. More significant, five of them were war orphans or refugees who had lived through harrowing wilderness experiences, including the murder of their own family members. Could these young women and slaves, who were grieving their lost loved ones and fearing for their futures, have been acting out their own personal traumas?

If their emotional breakdowns were exploited by friends and neighbors—not to mention the judges—as a vehicle for their own grievances, it was because the colony itself was broken. The afflicted girls, then, might have been the proverbial canary in the coal mine.

One of the single most important triggers of the crisis probably came down to the day in 1686 when the English monarchy annulled the Massachusetts charter. More than a mere legal document, it had been a constitution, guaranteeing the colonists' fundamental rights. Until it was restored six years later, New England lost its moorings. Those who had put their life earnings into a house and land now found it swept from underneath them, relinquished to the Crown. The courts were virtually shut down, elections postponed, and the governing body, the General Court, forbidden to assemble.

The more unscrupulous members of society exploited this legal breach. Without the deterrent of a functioning legal system, they could do as they pleased. In Salem, John Trask pilfered and then claimed title to Judge Corwin's farm, though Trask's father had sold it years before. In Andover, Benjamin Abbot revived an old boundary dispute with Martha Carrier that might otherwise have been forgotten. At her witchcraft hearing, he eagerly dredged up years of accumulated grudges to prove her malefic powers.

By the time Increase Mather dropped anchor in Boston with the new charter in hand, Massachusetts had turned itself inside out. Freed of legal constraints, the colonists had broken the moral ones, too, in a spasm of backstabbing and finger-pointing. Purging their neighborhoods of undesirables was a way to address the wrongs, something within their power. So much else was not.

Yet even after cleansing the "evil" from their midst, their troubles weren't over. They would still be prone to Indian atrocities, crop failures, infant deaths, and smallpox. Their property rights and their political leadership would still depend largely on London's whims. Fires would swallow their houses, as it had William Hooper's. There was no guarantee of survival—not to mention heavenly salvation—even for the saintly.

Mary Taylor would say as much at her Salem examination. What had made her turn to witchcraft? She fell silent, then bid the court to pray that she might speak the truth. A greater force had driven her to it, she said, "the Devil that guides destiny."

ACKN⊕WLEDGMENTS

I am grateful to Juliet Haines Mofford for her encouragement and support, and for steering me to invaluable sources. I also owe a big thanks to Carol Majahad, executive director of the North Andover Historical Society, for clearing up a puzzling enigma just in the nick of time. Most of all I'm beholden to Joseph Citro for keeping me going throughout, especially in the last frantic weeks. I couldn't have done it without him.

SALEM-AREA ACCUSERS

Name	Age	Town
1. Alice Booth	14	Salem
2. Elizabeth Booth	18	Salem
3. Richard Carrier	18	Andover
4. Sarah Churchill	25?	Salem
5. John DeRich	16	Salem
6. Rose Foster	13	Andover
7. Abigail Hobbs	?	Topsfield
8. Deliverance Hobbs	?	Topsfield
9. Elizabeth Hubbard	17	Salem Village
10. John Indian	?	Salem Village
11. Mercy Lewis	19	Salem Village
12. Abigail Martin	19	Salem Village
13. Mary Marshall	?	Andover
14. Elizabeth Parris	9	Reading
15. Sarah Phelps	12	Andover
16. Ann Putnam Jr.	12	Salem Village
17. Ann Putnam Sr.	30	Salem Village
18. Margaret Rule	17	Boston
19. Susannah Sheldon	18	Salem Village
20. Mercy Short	17	Boston
21. Martha Sprague	16	Andover
22. Timothy Swan	30	Andover
23. Sarah Vibber	36	?
24. Mary Walcott	17	Salem Village
25. Mary Warren	20	Salem
26. Mary Watkins	20s	Milton
27. Abigail Williams	12	Salem Village

SALEM-AREA ACCUSED*

EXECUTED

Name	Age	Town
1. Bridget Bishop	50s	Salem
2. George Burroughs	42?	Wells
3. Martha Carrier	40s	Andover
4. Giles Corey	70s	Salem
5. Martha Corey	70s?	Salem
6. Mary Easty	56	Topsfield
7. Sarah Good	38	Salem Village
8. Elizabeth Howe	50s	Topsfield
9. George Jacobs Sr.	80s	Salem
10. Susannah Martin	71	Amesbury
11. Rebecca Nurse	71	Salem Village
12. Alice Parker	?	Salem
13. Mary Parker	55	Andover
14. John Proctor	60	Salem Village
15. Ann Pudeator	70	Salem
16. Wilmot Reed	50s	Marblehead
17. Margaret Scott	77	Rowley
18. Samuel Wardwell	49	Andover
19. Sarah Wildes	65	Topsfield
20. John Willard	20s	Salem Village

DIED IN PRISON

Name	Age	Town
1. Lydia Dustin	79	Reading
2. Ann Foster	70s	Andover
3. Sarah Good's newborn	infant	Salem Village
4. Sarah Osborne	40s	Salem Village
5. Roger Toothaker	58	Billerica

*Dozens more were named but never arrested. This list does not include witchcraft cases in Connecticut.

ACCUSED

1.	Arthur Abbott	50s?	east of Salem
2.	Nehemiah Abbott	50s?	Topsfield
3.	Captain John Alden	60s	Boston
4.	Daniel Andrews	49	Salem Village
5.	Abigail Barker	36	Andover
6.	Mary Barker	13	Andover
7.	William Barker Sr.	46	Andover
8.	William Barker Jr.	14	Andover
9.	Sarah Bassett	35	Lynn
10.	Edward Bishop	40s	Salem Village
11.	Sarah Bishop	40s	Salem Village
12.	Mary Black (slave)	?	Salem Village
13.	Mary Bradbury	80s	Salisbury
14.	Ann Bradstreet	40s	Andover
15.	Col. Dudley Bradstreet	44	Andover
16.	John Bradstreet	40	Andover
17.	Mary Bridges Sr.	48	Andover
18.	Mary Bridges Jr.	12	Andover
19.	Sarah Bridges	20s	Andover
20.	Hannah Broomage	50s	Haverhill
21.	Sarah Buckley	55?	Salem Village
22.	John Busse	52	Boston
23.	Candy (slave)	?	Salem
24.	Andrew Carrier	15	Andover
25.	Richard Carrier	18	Andover
26.	Sarah Carrier	7	Andover
27.	Thomas Carrier Jr.	10	Andover
28.	Hannah Carroll	?	Salem
29.	Bethia Carter Sr.	40s	Woburn
30.	Bethia Carter Jr.	21	Woburn
31.	Elizabeth Cary	50s	Watertown
32.	Sarah Churchill	20	Salem
33.	Mary Clark	?	Haverhill
34.	Rachel Clenton	63	Ipswich

35. Sarah Cloyce	54	Topsfield
36. Sarah Cole	34	Lynn
37. Elizabeth Coleson	16	Reading
38. Mary Coleson	42	Reading
39. Deliverance Dane	41	Andover
40. Phebe Day	35	Gloucester
41. Bridget Denmark	20s	Boston
42. Mary DeRich	37	Salem Village
43. Elizabeth Dicer	40s?	Gloucester
44. Rebecca Dike	50s	Gloucester
45. Ann Dolliver	40?	Salem
46. Mehitable Downing	40	Ipswich
47. Joseph Draper	21	Andover
48. Sarah Dustin	39	Reading
49. Daniel Eames	28	Boxford
50. Rebecca Eames	51	Boxford
51. Esther Elwell	53	Gloucester
52. Martha Emerson	24	Haverhill
53. Joseph Emmons	40s	Manchester
54. Mary English	39	Salem
55. Philip English	41	Salem
56. Thomas Farrar Sr.	75	Lynn
57. Edward Farrington	30	Andover
58. Abigail Faulkner Sr.	40	Andover
59. Abigail Faulkner Jr.	8	Andover
60. Dorothy Faulkner	10	Andover
61. Capt. John Flood	50s	Rumney Marsh
62. Elizabeth Fosdick	36	Malden
63. Eunice Fry	50	Andover
64. Dorothy Good	4	Salem Village
65. Mary Green	30s	Haverhill
66. Sarah Hale	36	Beverly
67. Elizabeth Hart	70	Lynn
68. Margaret Hawkes	40s?	Salem
69. Sarah Hawkes	21	Andover
70. Dorcas Hoar	50s	Beverly
71. Abigail Hobbs	15	Topsfield

72. Deliverance Hobbs	40s?	Topsfield
73. William Hobbs	50	Topsfield
74. James Howe	50s	Ipswich
75. John Howard	30s	Rowley
76. Frances Hutchins	60s	Haverhill
77. Mary Ireson	50s	Lynn
78. John Jackson Sr.	50s	Rowley
79. John Jackson Jr.	22	Rowley
80. Margaret Jacobs	17	Salem
81. Rebecca Jacobs	46	Salem Village
82. Abigail Johnson	11	Andover
83. Elizabeth Johnson Sr.	50	Andover
84. Rebecca Johnson Jr.	17	Andover
85. Rebecca Johnson Sr.	50	Andover
86. Stephen Johnson	13	Andover
87. Mary Lacey Sr.	40	Andover
88. Mary Lacey Jr.	18	Andover
89. Jane Lilly	?	Reading
90. Mary Morey	?	Beverly
91. Sarah Parker	14	Andover
92. Elizabeth Paine	53	Malden
93. Sarah Pease	?	Salem
94. Joan Penney	?	Gloucester
95. Hannah Post	30s	Boxford
96. Mary Post	28	Rowley
97. Susanna Post	26	Andover
98. Margaret Prince	66	Gloucester
99. Benjamin Proctor	33	Salem
100. Elizabeth Proctor	40s	Salem
101. Sarah Proctor	16	Salem
102. William Proctor	17	Salem
103. Sarah Rice	?	Reading
104. Abigail Roe	15	Gloucester
105. Mary Roe	34	Gloucester
106. Susanna Roots	?	Beverly
107. Henry Salter	?	Andover
108. John Sawdey	13	Andover

109. Ann Sears	?	Woburn
110. Susanna Sheldon	18	Salem
111. Abigail Soames	37	Salem
112. Martha Sparkes	36	Chelmsford
113. Mary Taylor	40s	Reading
114. Tituba	?	Salem Village
115. Job Tookey	20s	Beverly
116. Margaret Toothaker	9	Billerica
117. Mary Toothaker	48	Billerica
118. Hannah Tyler	13	Andover
119. Johanna Tyler	12	Andover
120. Martha Tyler	16	Andover
121. Mary Tyler	35	Andover
122. Hezekiah Usher	53	Boston
123. Sarah Vincent	60s	Gloucester
124. Mercy Wardwell	19	Andover
125. Sarah Wardwell	41	Andover
126. Mary Warren	20	Salem Village
127. Mary Watkins	20s	Milton
128. Ruth Wilford	?	Haverhill
129. Sarah Wilson Jr.	?	Andover
130. Sarah Wilson Sr.	40s	Andover
131. Mary Witheridge	40	Salem Village

N⊕TES

1. As Rosenthal points out in *Records of the Salem Witch-Hunt,* most historians now feel that when Reverend John Hale wrote of this egg and coffin episode, he was referring to an event that occurred outside the framework of the Salem Village witch hunt.

CHAP+ER I, THE ACCUSERS

1. For insight into the social connections between the afflicted girls, see page 287 of Frances Hill's book, *The Salem Witch Trials Reader.*

CHAP+ER 2, THE VIC+IMS

1. In *The Devil in the Shape of a Woman,* Karlsen offers a look at how economic factors predisposed a woman to suspicion.

2. In his book *Salem Story,* Rosenthal offers a convincing argument that the Boston clerical leadership's determination to convict George Burroughs was based on their belief that he was a Baptist, which they viewed as an unacceptable deviation from their own orthodox Congregationalism. Burroughs's punishment, Rosenthal believes, was meant as a warning to other nonconformist clerics.

3. In *The Foster Genealogy,* vol. 2, Pierce paints a full portrait of Ann Foster's family circumstances.

4. For an account of the Hannah Stone murder, see page 25 of Mofford's book *Andover Massachusetts.*

5. According to family legend, George Jacobs Sr.'s remains were secretly removed from the common grave at Gallows Hill and spirited back to his farm for a Christian burial. In the mid-nineteenth century, after the farm lay abandoned, a

grave presumed to be his was uncovered there. The bones
were removed in the 1950s and kept in storage. In 1992
Salem's tercentennial committee arranged a quiet funeral
and interment near Rebecca Nurse's grave in the small
cemetery behind the Rebecca Nurse Homestead in Danvers,
Massachusetts, which is now a museum.

6. Part 3 of Williams and Adelman's book, *Riding the Nightmare,*
   contains an interesting summary of Sarah Osborne's
   victimization.

7. An overview of Mary Parker's extended family is given on
   page 251 of Robinson's *Salem Witchcraft.*

8. See chapter 2 of Peterson's *Marblehead* for a summary of
   Wilmot Reed's predicament. In his 1881 tome, *The History
   and Traditions of Marblehead,* Roads offers a full account of the
   local quarrels that resulted in Wilmot Reed's conviction.

9. See Rice's paper, "Spectors, Maleficium and Margaret Scott,"
   for a detailed description of the Rowley widow's ostracism.

10. Robinson gives an in-depth account of Samuel Wardwell's
    background in chapter 5 of his book, *Salem Witchcraft.*

11. Mary Gould Reddington should have saved her indignation
    for John Herrick, her dissolute son-in-law. Sometime around
    1691, Herrick not only deserted his wife, Bethia, and their
    two children, but made off with her money. Bethia's sister
    took her in, but the arrangement was short-lived when her
    brother-in-law couldn't keep his hands off her. Had Bethia not
    been in such a fix, she might have lent a hand to her other
    sister, Sarah Good. As it was, Salem solved Sarah's problem by
    executing the homeless woman for witchcraft.

12. A detailed overview of the Wilkins clan of Salem Village,
    including its Welsh ancestry, is included in Cutter's *New
    England Families,* p. 193.

13. For a firsthand account of the August 19 execution, see
    Calef's tome, *More Wonders of the Invisible World.*

CHAPTER 3, THE CLERGY

1. Barnard's saltbox-style parsonage at 179 Osgood Street, rebuilt in 1715 after a fire destroyed his first home, is now a museum. In 1692 Andover's meetinghouse was located on the triangular spot directly across the road from the cemetery. The Simon Bradstreet house is thought to have stood on the green, south of the cemetery, or just west of the green.

2. The grave of Reverend Thomas Barnard still stands in what is now North Andover, where Academy Road crosses Court Street. Its epitaph reads as follows: Here Lyes Buried ye Body of ye Revernd Mr Thomas Barnard Who Departed this Life Octor 13th Anno Domi 1718 AEtatis Suae 62. Though the epitaph puts his age at sixty-two, his son John Barnard would write in his diary that his father died at age sixty. The same age is cited in volume 3 of Sibley's *Biographical Sketches of Graduates of Harvard University*.

3. Robinson lays out the complex intermarriage of the Dane and Chandler families on pages 224–225 of his book, *Salem Witchcraft and Hawthorne's House of the Seven Gables*. To wit, the two families had been close both in England and Massachusetts. Having both settled in Ipswich, Francis Dane's widowed father married Hannah Chandler's widowed mother in 1642. Then in 1658, Hannah's brother William married the daughter of Francis Dane's brother, Mary Dane. Francis Dane's 1690 marriage to Hannah Chandler Abbot would be the third time that the two families intermarried.

4. The house where Reverend John Hale lived from 1694 until his death in 1700 is now a museum, the John Hale House, at 39 Hale Street in Beverly, Massachusetts. Hale is buried with his wives in the nearby graveyard, in the Hale family plot.

5. Increase Mather's parsonage was on the site of what today is the historic Paul Revere House, a museum at 19 North Square, Boston. Though completely rebuilt in 1680 after it had burned, the house probably looked very much as it does today, with its second-story overhang, diamond-shaped window panes, low ceilings, and sparse furnishings.

6. The 1693 publication's full name was: *Cases of Conscience concerning evil Spirits Personating Men, Witchcrafts, infallible Proofs of Guilt in such as are accused of that Crime. All Considered according to the Scriptures, History, Experience, and the Judgment of many Learned men.*

CHAP+ER 4, THE JUDGES

1. New England's magistrates were merchants first, judges second. The full magnitude of their business dealings is outlined in Martin's book, *Profits in the Wilderness.*

2. Ruth Gardner Hathorne's parents were Lieutenant George Gardner and Elizabeth Freestone Turner Gardner. Her mother was the fervent Quaker, having immigrated to Massachusetts to be near the controversial Anne Hutchinson. Elizabeth Gardner's name shows up in early criminal records for skipping out on Sunday services, which in those days was a punishable offense. With her first husband, Boston shoemaker John Turner, she gave birth to their son John Turner, who would own Salem's famous House of the Seven Gables. Though Ruth Hathorne's father did not share her mother's Quaker beliefs, it was his responsibility to pay her fines. The couple fled to Hartford, Connecticut, to avoid persecution. In her book, *The Salem World of Nathaniel Hawthorne,* Moore writes on page 33 that in his will, Gardner left the couple's Connecticut debts to their considerably better-heeled daughter.

3. Saltonstall left his generously endowed estate to his four children, all but the youngest of whom survived him. His eldest, Gurdon Saltonstall, would become a Connecticut governor. Another six generations of Saltonstalls followed in his footsteps as Harvard graduates and public servants.

4. Andros had surrounded himself with royal appointees and other like-minded Englishmen who gave little thought to the economic interests of New England merchants. As Harvard historian Bailyn makes clear in his book, *The New England Merchants in the Seventeenth Century,* such Massachusetts ship owners as Sergeant, John Richards, Samuel Shrimpton, and Bartholomew Gedney banded together to depose him not

so much because he had not been democratically elected, but because he gave them little say in government policy. Under William Phips, Massachusetts would again be ruled by merchants.

5. Two years after Sergeant's death in 1714, his English Renaissance mansion was purchased by the Province of Massachusetts for 2,300 pounds and reincarnated as an official residence, housing a succession of royal governors. In 1922 the "Province House" was razed to make room for an office building and movie theater.

6. In her book, *Salem Witch Judge,* Sewall's twenty-first-century descendent Eve LaPlante likens it to a traditional cilice or hair shirt worn to induce atonement.

7. Samuel Sewall's grave can be visited in Boston at the Granary Burying Ground on Tremont Street.

CHAPTER 5. THE ELITE

1. A descendent, Alvah Bradstreet, wrote about Simon Bradstreet's property acquisitions on a Christmas card in 1956 that years later was reprinted in the Massachusetts Institute of Technology's publication "Danvers Senior Oracle." The future governor, it seems, was so envious upon learning that Massachusetts Bay Colony Governor John Endicott had won himself a land grant in Salem, that he requested one for himself. He received five hundred acres, starting at Endicott's property line and stretching toward Topsfield. He never used it, but left the tract to his son John, who married the daughter of Topsfield's minister. According to the same source, Simon Bradstreet also purchased "a large tract of land in the upper part" of Essex County, paying the Indians "ten dollars [probably pounds], an old coat, and some small trinkets."

2. Anne Dudley Bradstreet's brother-in-law, John Woodbridge, was Andover's first minister. He returned to England in 1647, taking with him Anne's poetry, which would be published in London three years later as *The Tenth Muse, Lately Sprung Up in America.* Anne Bradstreet is considered America's first major poet.

267

3. In Charles Upham's opinion, had Simon Bradstreet stayed on as the colony's governor, he would have nipped the witch hunt in the bud. Upham served both as Salem's mayor and as its minister, but he was first and foremost a historian. His life's work was to publish the first comprehensive history of the Salem witch trials. *Salem Witchcraft,* which came out in 1867, is still regarded as one of the best.

4. The full name of Brattle's 1692 missive is "A Letter giving a full and candid account of the Delusion called Witchcraft, which prevailed in New England, and of the Judicial Trials and Executions at Salem, in the County of Essex, for that pretended Crime in 1692."

5. Sibley writes in volume 2 of his book on Harvard graduates that its "loud noise" was not to everyone's liking. In 1713 the church voted to decline the gift, as the members did "not think it proper to use ye same in ye publick worship of God." A month later, the "gentlemen of the church" reconsidered. An English organist was procured at thirty pounds per annum, and soon after, organ music blared over the Boston congregation. It would be the first in a New England church.

6. From an online biography by Anne Calef Boardman, http:// familypedia.wikia.com/wiki/Robert_Calef_(1648–1719).

7. Danforth's third and last surviving son, according to Sibley's book, was Jonathan Danforth, who died in 1682 at the age of twenty-two while studying at Harvard.

8. Samuel Sewall writes in his diary that Danforth died of "consumption."

9. Reverend Cotton Mather would write that Phips was one of twenty-six children, a gross exaggeration. After the death of Phips's father, his mother would remarry and bear another eight offspring, for a total of fourteen.

10. Sir William Phips's grave can be visited in the yard of the (Anglican) Church of St. Mary Woolnoth, on the corner of Lombard and King William Streets in London.

BIBLI⊕GRAPHY

Babson, John J. *Notes and Additions to the History of Gloucester*. Charleston, SC: BiblioLife, 2009.

Bailey, Sarah Loring. *Historical Sketches of Andover, comprising the present towns of North Andover and Andover, Massachusetts.* Boston: Houghton Mifflin and Company, 1880.

Bailyn, Bernard. *The New England Merchants in the Seventeenth Century.* Cambridge, MA: Harvard University Press, 1979.

Baker, Emerson W., and James Kences. "Indian Land Speculation and the Essex County Witchcraft Outbreak of 1692." *Maine History*, Vol. 40, No. 3, Fall 2001, pp. 159–189.

Boyer, Paul, and Stephen Nissenbaum, editors. *Salem-Village Witchcraft: A Documentary Record of Local Conflict in Colonial New England.* Boston: Northeastern University Press, 1972.

———. *Salem Possessed: The Social Origins of Witchcraft.* Cambridge, MA: Harvard University Press, 1974.

Burr, George Lincoln, editor. *Narratives of the Witchcraft Cases, 1646–1706.* New York: Barnes & Noble, 1972.

Calef, Robert. *More Wonders of the Invisible World.* London: Printed for Nath. Hillar, at the Princess-Arms, in Leaden-Hall-Street, over against St. Mary-Ax, and Joseph Collier, at the Golden Bible, on London Bridge, 1700.

Carpenter, Edmund J. "The Province House." *The New England Magazine,* Vol. 21, by Making of America Project. Boston: Warren F. Kellogg, Publisher, September 1899–February 1900.

Cutter, William Richard, editor. *New England Families, Genealogical and Memorial: A Record of the Achievements of Her People in the Making of Commonwealths and the Founding of a Nation*. Vol. 1. New York: Lewis Historical Publishing Company, 1915.

Demos, John. *Entertaining Satan: Witchcraft and the Culture of Early New England*. New York: Oxford University Press, 1982.

——. *The Enemy Within: 2,000 Years of Witch-Hunting in the Western World*. New York: Viking, 2008.

Dunham, Peter C., editor. *Genealogies and Family Histories of Some Ancestors and Descendents of Leslie Aaron Carrier and Blanche Evelina French*. Ashland, MA: private issue, 2008.

Erickson, Carolly. *Royal Panoply: Brief Lives of the English Monarchs*. New York: History Book Club, 2003.

Gordon, Charlotte. *Mistress Bradstreet: The Untold Life of America's First Poet*. New York: Little, Brown and Company, 2005.

Goss, K. David. *The Salem Witch Trials: A Reference Guide*. Westport, CT: Greenwood Publishing Group, 2007.

Hall, David D., editor. *Witch-Hunting in Seventeenth-Century New England: A Documentary History, 1638–1692*. Boston: Northeastern University Press, 1991.

——. *Worlds of Wonder, Days of Judgment: Popular Religious Belief in Early New England*. Cambridge, MA: Harvard University Press, 1989.

Heyrman Christine. *Commerce and Culture: The Maritime Communities of Colonial Massachusetts, 1690–1750*. New York: W. W. Norton & Co., 1986.

Hill, Frances. *The Salem Witch Trials Reader*. Cambridge, MA: Da Capo Press, 2000.

Hill, Hamilton Andrews, and Appleton Prentiss Clark Griffin. *History of the Old South Church Boston, 1669–1884.* Vol. 1. Cambridge, MA: The Riverside Press, 1890.

An Historical Catalogue of the Old South Church (Third Church), Boston. Boston: printed for private distribution, press of David Clapp & Son, 1883.

Hunter, Phyllis Whitman. *Purchasing Identity in the Atlantic World: Massachusetts Merchants, 1670–1780.* Ithaca, NY: Cornell University Press, 2001.

Karlsen, Carol F. *The Devil in the Shape of a Woman: Witchcraft in Colonial New England.* New York: W. W. Norton & Co., 1987.

LaPlante, Eve. *Salem Witch Judge: The Life and Repentance of Samuel Sewall.* New York: HarperCollins, 2007.

Martin, John Frederick. *Profits in the Wilderness: Entrepreneurship and the Founding of New England Towns in the Seventeenth Century.* Chapel Hill: The University of North Carolina Press, 1991.

Mofford, Juliet Haines. *And Firm Thine Ancient Vow: The History of North Parish Church of North Andover, 1645–1974.* North Andover, MA: The Naiman Press, Inc., 1975.

——. *Andover Massachusetts: Historical Selections from Four Centuries.* Andover, MA: Merrimack Valley Preservation Press, 2004.

Moore, Margaret B. *The Salem World of Nathaniel Hawthorne.* Columbus: University of Missouri Press, 1998.

Norton, Mary Beth. *In the Devil's Snare: The Salem Witchcraft Crisis of 1692.* New York: Alfred A. Knopf, 2002.

Peterson, Mark A. *The Price of Redemption: The Spiritual Economy of Puritan New England.* Stanford, CA: Stanford University Press, 1997.

Peterson, Pam Matthias. *Marblehead: Myths, Legends and Lore from Storied Past to Modern Mystery.* Charleston, SC: The History Press, 2007.

Pierce, Frederick Clifton. *The Foster Genealogy.* Vol. 2. Chicago: W. B. Conkey Company, 1899.

Rice, Mark. "Spectors, Maleficium and Margaret Scott." Paper written at Cornell University in 2003 and revised for presentation in 2005 at the Berkshire Conference of Women Historians in Amherst, MA. Online at www2.iath.virginia.edu/saxon-salem/servlet/SaxonServlet?source=salem/texts/bios.xml&style=salem/xsl/dynaxml.xsl&chunk.id=b43&clear-stylesheet-cache=yes.

Roach, Marilynne K. *The Salem Witchcraft Trials.* Lanham, MD: Taylor Trade Publishing, 2004.

———. *In the Days of the Salem Witchcraft Trials.* Boston: Houghton Mifflin Co., 1996.

Roads, Samuel. *The History and Traditions of Marblehead.* Boston: Houghton Mifflin Co., 1881.

Robinson, Enders. *Salem Witchcraft and Hawthorne's House of the Seven Gables.* Bowie, MD: Heritage Books, 1992.

Rosenthal, Bernard, editor. *Records of the Salem Witch-Hunt.* Cambridge: Cambridge University Press, 2009.

———. *Salem Story: Reading the Witch Trials of 1692.* Cambridge: Cambridge University Press, 1993.

Savage, James. *A Genealogical Dictionary of the First Settlers of New England, showing three generations of those who came before May, 1692, on the basis of Farmer's Register.* Vol. 4. Boston: Little, Brown and Company, 1862.

Sibley, John Langdon. *Biographical Sketches of Graduates of Harvard University in Cambridge, Massachusetts.* Vol. 1–3, 1678–1689. Cambridge: Cambridge University Press, 1873; Boston: John Wilson & Son, 1885.

Slotkin, Richard. *Regeneration through Violence: The Mythology of the American Frontier, 1600–1860.* Norman: University of Oklahoma Press, 2000.

Upham, Charles W. *Salem Witchraft; with an account of Salem Village, and a history of opinions on witchcraft and kindred subjects.* Vol. I & II. Boston: Wiggin and Lunt, 1867.

Watkins, Walter Kendall. "The Province House and Its Occupants." Edited by Richard M. Candee. http://spnea.org/resources/articles/pdf195.pdf.

Williams, Selma R., and Pamela Williams Adelman. *Riding the Nightmare: Women & Witchcraft from the Old World to Colonial Salem.* New York: Harper Perennial, 1978.

The Winthrop Papers, Collections of the Massachusetts Historical Society, 1892.

INDEX

AB⊕UT THE AUTH⊕R

Diane E. Foulds has spent ten years in the research of seventeenth-century Massachusetts for clues into the life of her ancestor, who was one of the nineteen hanged. A journalist and writer, she has worked in Montreal, Vienna, Moscow, and Prague, contributing to a variety of U.S. and European publications. This is her fourth book.

CPSIA information can be obtained
at www.ICGtesting.com
Printed in the USA
BVHW080019120921
616417BV00003B/5